Hank Janson
Under Cover
A Visual History

OVER 8 MILLION SALE!

Read HANK JANSON

FIRST SERIES

1. THIS WOMAN IS DEATH
2. LADY, MIND THAT CORPSE
3. GUN MOLL FOR HIRE
4. NO REGRETS FOR CLARA
5. SMART GIRLS DON'T TALK
6. LILIES FOR MY LOVELY
7. BLONDE ON THE SPOT
8. HONEY, TAKE MY GUN
9. SWEETHEART, HERE'S YOUR GRAVE
10. GUNSMOKE IN HER EYES
11. ANGEL, SHOOT TO KILL
12. SLAY-RIDE FOR CUTIE

SECOND SERIES

13. SISTER, DON'T HATE ME
14. SOME LOOK BETTER DEAD
15. SWEETIE, HOLD ME TIGHT
16. TORMENT FOR TRIXIE
17. DON'T DARE ME, SUGAR
18. THE LADY HAS A SCAR
19. THE JANE WITH GREEN EYES
20. LOLA BROUGHT HER WREATH
21. LADY TOLL THE BELL
22. THE BRIDE WORE WEEDS
23. DON'T MOURN ME TOOTS
24. THIS DAME DIES SOON

THIRD SERIES

25. BABY, DON'T DARE SQUEAL
26. DEATH WORE A PETTICOAT
27. HOTSY, YOU'LL BE CHILLED
28. IT'S ALWAYS EVE THAT WEEPS
29. FRAILS CAN BE SO TOUGH
30. MILADY TOOK THE RAP
31. WOMEN HATE TILL DEATH
32. BROADS DON'T SCARE EASY
33. SKIRTS BRING ME SORROW
34. SADIE, DONT CRY NOW
35. THE FILLY WORE A ROD
36. KILL HER IF YOU CAN

FOURTH SERIES

37. MURDER
38. CONFLICT
39. TENSION
40. WHIPLASH
41. ACCUSED
42. KILLER
43. SUSPENSE
44. PURSUIT
45. VENGEANCE
46. TORMENT
47. AMOK
48. CORRUPTION (In preparation)

SPECIALS

(a) AUCTIONED
(b) PERSIAN PRIDE
(c) DESERT FURY (In preparation)
(d) UNSEEN ASSASSIN ,,
(e) ONE MAN IN HIS TIME (In preparation)

ON SALE EVERYWHERE Price 2/-

In case of difficulty write to the Sole Distributors:
GAYWOOD PRESS LIMITED
30 GAYWOOD STREET, LONDON, S.E.1

Hank Janson
Under Cover
A Visual History

Stephen James Walker

First published in England by:
Telos Publishing Ltd
139 Whitstable Road, Canterbury, Kent CT2 8EQ, UK
www.telos.co.uk

Telos Publishing Ltd values feedback. Please e-mail any comments you might have about this book to: feedback@telos.co.uk.

ISBN: 978-1-84583-165-3

© 2021 Stephen James Walker

The moral right of the author has been asserted.

Design, typesetting and layout by Stephen James Walker.

Printed in India by Imprint Press.

The Hank Janson name, logo and silhouette device are registered trademarks of Telos Publishing Ltd.

British Library Cataloguing in Publication Data.
A catalogue record for this book is available from the British Library.

This book is sold subject to the condition that it shall not, by way of trade or otherwise, be lent, resold, hired out or otherwise circulated without the publisher's prior written consent in any form of binding or cover other than that in which it is published and without a similar condition including this condition being imposed on the subsequent purchaser.

Dedicated to Steve Holland.

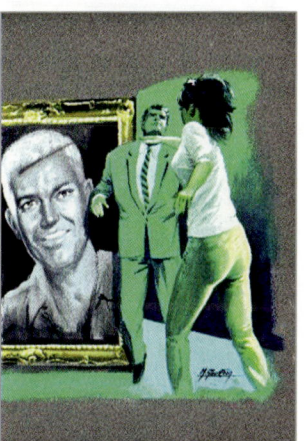

Above: artist Michel Gourdon's original paintings for the French-language Hank Janson editions *Intoxicomani* (left), *Fan-Fanfare* (top right) and *Vaudou Veau d'Or* (bottom right), published by Editions 'Fleuve Noir' in 1972, 1966 and 1967 respectively (see page 221).

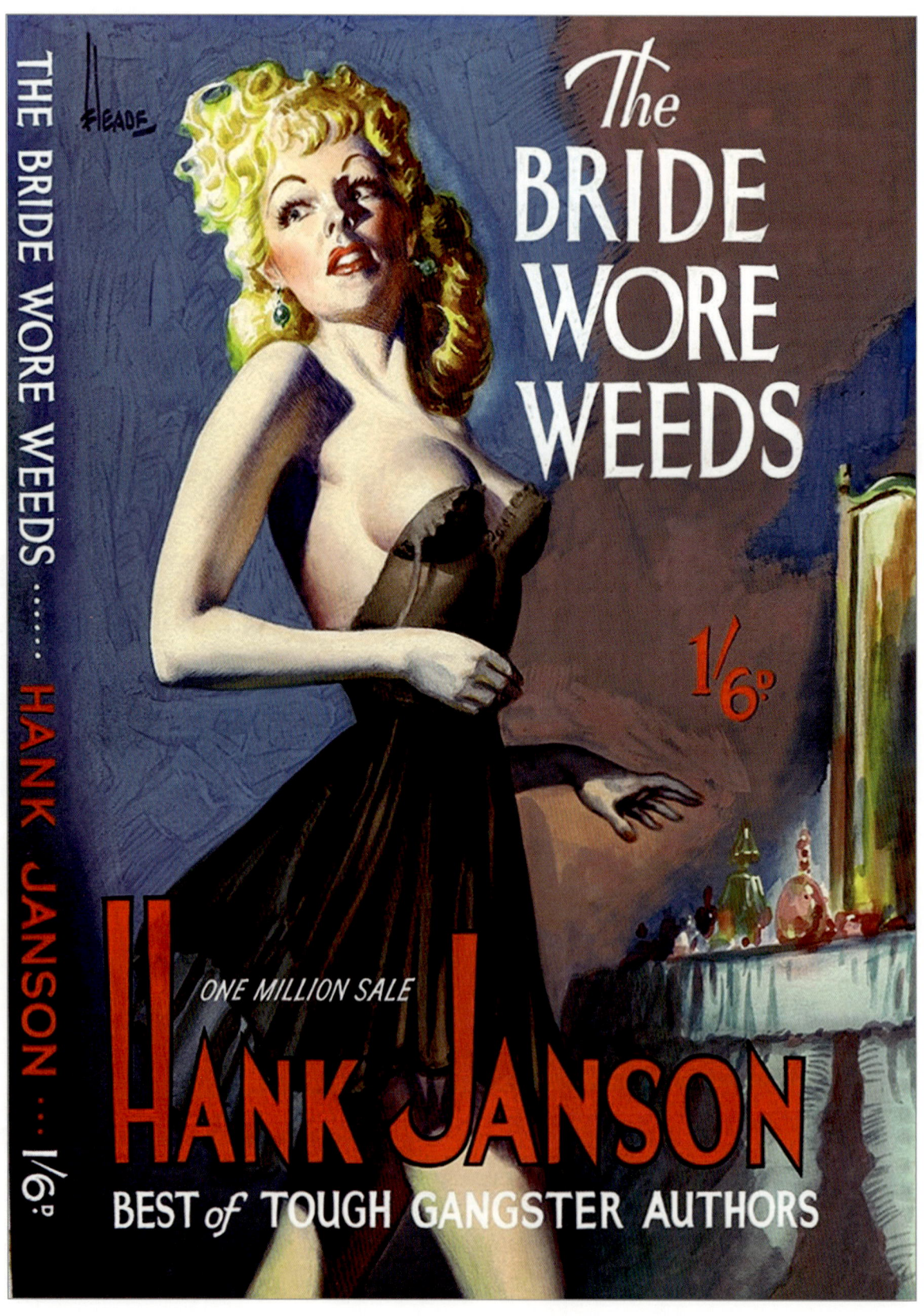

Reginald Heade's original cover painting for *The Bride Wore Weeds* (S D Frances, December 1950). The visible brush-marks were smoothed out on the as-printed version (see page 40). As with most of his covers prior to the mid-1950s, the artist had to provide all the lettering himself.

CONTENTS

Introduction 9

The Classic Era 13

Silhouette Cover Reissues 95

Alexander Moring 103

Roberts & Vinter 125

Compact 159

Compact Reissues 197

Hilary Brand 205

North American Editions 211

Foreign-Language Editions 219

Revivals 253

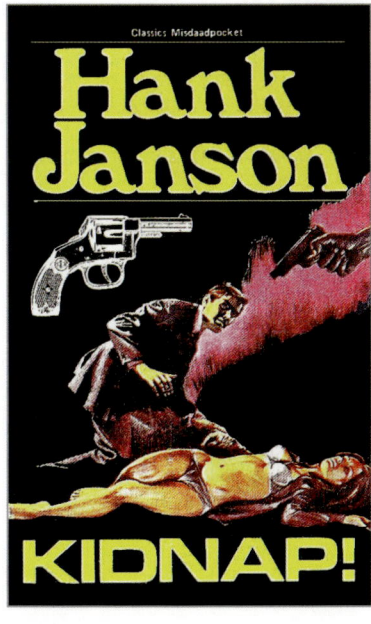  

Three of the many foreign-language Hank Janson translations, these ones coming from (left to right) the Netherlands, Denmark and Germany. (Further information in the section beginning on page 219.)

When Dames Get Tough (Ward & Hitchon, 1946) – the very first Hank Janson book, a slim, 24-page novelette. Cover art probably by Bob Wilkin. (Image courtesy Steve Holland.)

INTRODUCTION

With their hardboiled crime tales and sensational cover paintings of scantily-clad dames, the Hank Janson pulp paperbacks were a British publishing sensation in the late 1940s and early 1950s, being frequently reprinted and selling millions of copies to readers craving escapism from post-war austerity. Prosecutions under Britain's then-harsh obscenity laws dealt them a severe blow, however, and today those classic-era titles – published initially by the character's creator and principal author Stephen Frances, then by Reginald Carter through his New Fiction Press and Top Fiction Press – are highly sought-after by collectors.

In the mid-1950s, the range passed in turn to two more of Carter's companies, Alexander Moring and George Turton, and enjoyed further success. Then in 1959 the rights were sold on to a firm called Roberts & Vinter, which some three years later was taken over by entrepreneurs Godfrey Gold and David Warburton. But their Compact imprint titles saw sales slowly decline during the 1960s, until in 1971 the range finally met with cancellation.

Those wishing to read a full account of the Hank Janson story should seek out a copy of Steve Holland's excellent book *The Trials of Hank Janson* (Telos Publishing, 2005). *Hank Janson Under Cover* has a different aim: to present a complete visual history of the range. Particularly where the classic-era titles were concerned, the shamelessly erotic cover art, almost all of it supplied by the brilliant, unmatched Reginald Heade, was at least as important a part of the books' appeal as the stories within – if not more so. Heade's life and work have already been extensively detailed in the multi-volume *The Art of Reginald Heade* (Telos Publishing, 2016-2020), but *Hank Janson Under Cover* for the first time presents all of his wonderful Hank Janson pieces in full-page size, and in better quality than ever before. After Heade's time, the standard of the books' artwork became more variable, going into a steep decline in the mid-1960s and in the end even giving way to poorly-executed photographic compositions, but there were still some real gems produced by other artists, particularly Michel Atkinson. Even at their worst, those later covers retain a certain nostalgic appeal and period interest; and, again, *Hank Janson Under Cover* reproduces them all. To round things off, also pictured are many examples of the books' numerous non-UK editions.

I am delighted to have this opportunity to showcase, for readers' pleasure, the spectacular visual legacy of the Hank Janson phenomenon.

Stephen James Walker, July 2021

Above: the classic-era Hank Janson silhouette logo, designed by Philip Mendoza.

STEPHEN D FRANCES

Hank Janson was the pseudonym adopted by author Stephen D Frances when he created the Janson character and wrote the first of the books, *When Dames Get Tough*, in 1946. The name seemed to him to have the right 'hardboiled American' ring to it – 'Hank' was chosen as the forename mainly because it rhymed with 'Yank'!

Frances went on to write all of the classic-era Janson titles – bar perhaps one or two, over which experts disagree – and many of the later ones too, although almost all of those post-1959 were by different and arguably inferior authors, including Harry Hobson, Victor Norwood and Jim Moffatt.

Frances was born in 1917 in Lambeth, South London, and grew up in near poverty. A man of left-wing views, he was a conscientious objector during World War II. After trying out a number of different jobs and writing a few newspaper articles, he founded a small press, Pendulum Publications, in 1944. It was under that company's Ward & Hitchon imprint that *When Dames Get Tough*, and its follow-up *Scarred Faces*, appeared. The first few full Hank Janson novels, though, were published by a company under Frances's own name. Then he made a deal with publisher Reginald Carter, and the remainder of the classic-era books – subdivided into five regular series and a number of 'specials' – were issued by two of Carter's companies, New Fiction Press and Top Fiction Press, and distributed by Gaywood, a business owned by another Frances associate, Julius Reiter. In 1952, Frances actually sold all of the rights in Hank Janson to Carter, who continued publishing the range through his Alexander Moring press before he too sold it on.

The huge success of the books gave Frances a comfortable lifestyle and made him something of a minor celebrity – although on the few occasions when he was interviewed, he insisted on adopting the Janson persona and appearing 'under cover' in a mask and hat, to disguise the fact that he in no way resembled the Janson image! In the early 1950s he moved to Spain – a country for which he had a great affection. This was perhaps just as well, as it meant he escaped the main impact of the prosecutions brought against the Janson books at that time under the Obscene Publications Act, which resulted in both Carter and Reiter being jailed. On later returning to England, Frances was acquitted of all charges after claiming that he did not write the Janson books – which was strictly true, as he dictated them into a dictaphone and they were then transcribed by a typist!

Frances continued writing into the 1970s, although the last Hank Janson novel that can be reliably attributed to him was published in 1963. He died in 1989, at his home in Spain, of emphysema.

HANK JANSON

Whereas most of the male heroes of classic pulp crime fiction fell into the police detective or private eye mould, Hank Janson had a different line of work. In the two initial Ward & Hitchon titles he was a commercial salesman of beauty products for a New York-based company, but in the main classic-era novels he became ace crime reporter on the *Chicago Chronicle* newspaper.

The following is a fictional biography that appeared in a number of the books:

Hank Janson tells us that he was born in England during the Great War. There is very little of interest about his early school life except, perhaps, when at the age of fifteen, in order to win a wager with his school friends, he borrowed his brother's motor bike, which he had never previously driven, and entered himself for a cross-country endurance race. He smashed his brother's bike and wore his arm in a sling for months afterwards.

When he was nineteen, he stowed away on a fishing trawler and started on an adventure which was to last until 1945. Not once during the intervening years did he come back to England. He has dived for pearls in the Pacific, spent two years in the Arctic with a whaling fleet and worked his way through most of the American States. He obtained American nationality some years ago, worked in New York as a truck driver, news reporter and as assistant to a private detective agency. During the war he served in Burma.

Two years ago he returned to England and is now living in Surrey with his wife and children, spending his time gardening and writing about his personal experiences in a fictional form.

His life has been rich, exciting and dangerous – and almost, it may be said, as true to life as his stories.

Scarred Faces (Ward & Hitchon, 1946) – the second Hank Janson title. Cover art probably by Bob Wilkin. This 64-page book actually included two novelettes: *Scarred Faces* and *Kitty Takes the Rap*.

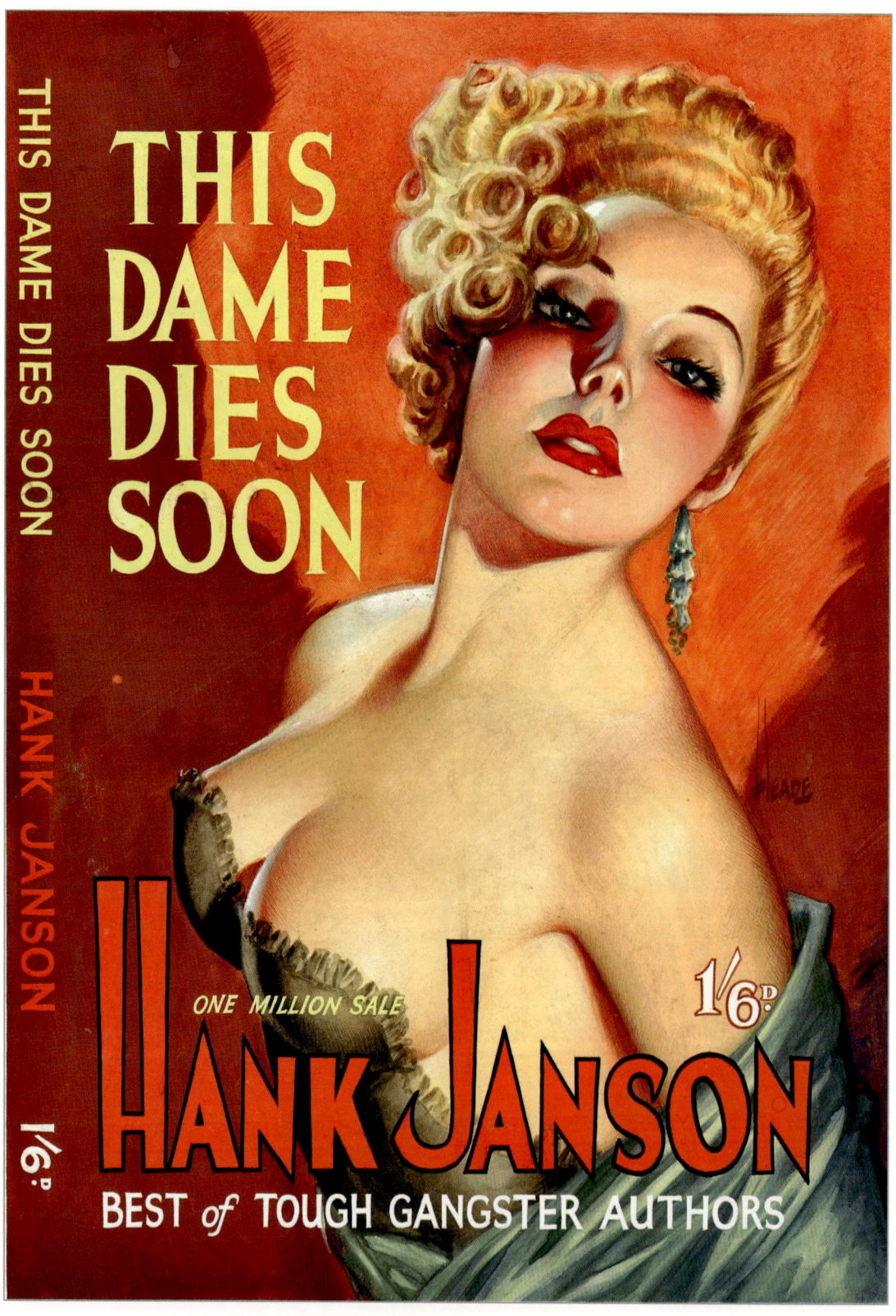

Reginald Heade's original cover painting for *This Dame Dies Soon* (S D Frances, February 1951), showing much greater detail and subtlety of colour than on the as-printed paperback (see page 42). (Image courtesy Rian Hughes.)

THE CLASSIC ERA

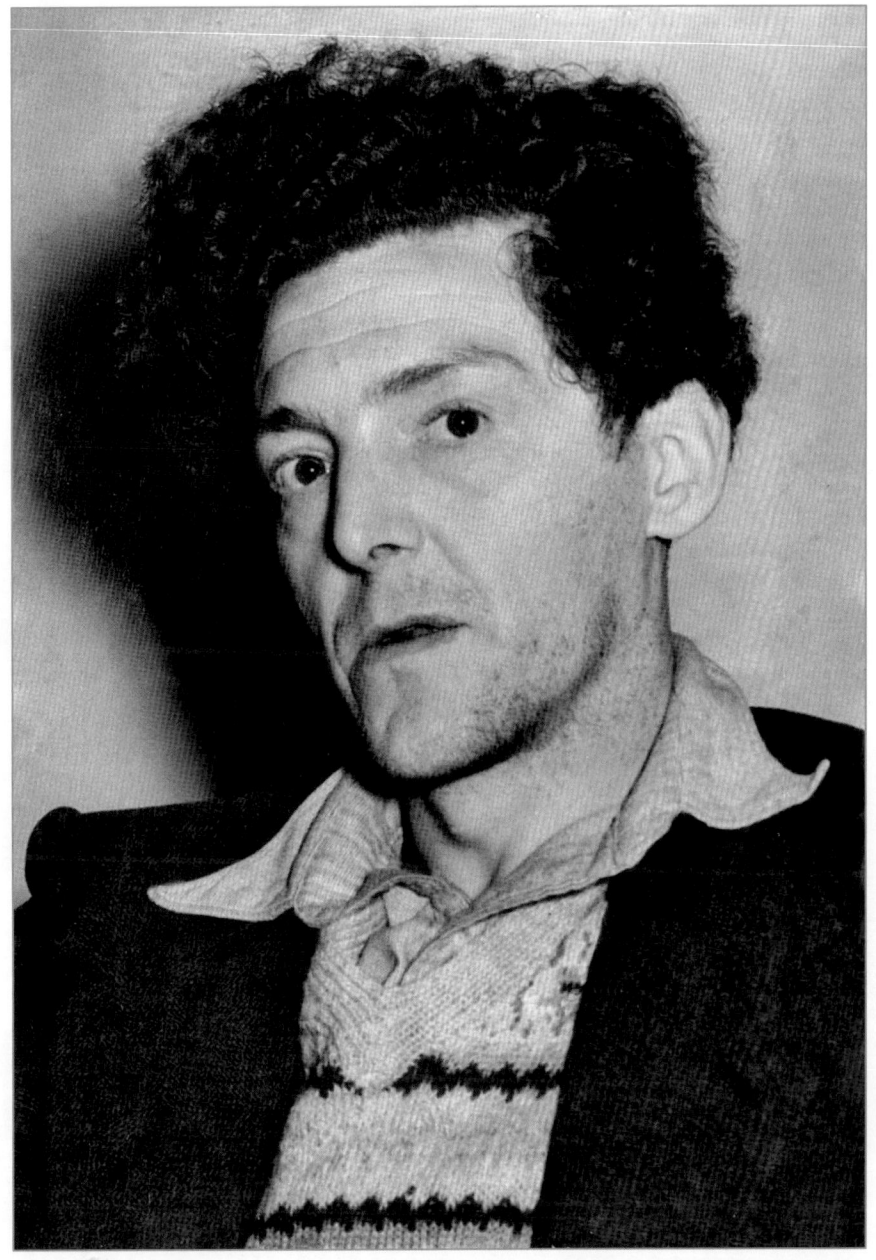

Hank Janson's creator and principal author, Stephen D Frances, pictured in 1954.

This Woman is Death (S D Frances, June 1948). Art by Reginald Heade. (Image courtesy Steve Holland.)

Lady, Mind That Corpse (S D Frances, September 1948). Art by Reginald Heade. (Image courtesy Steve Holland.)

Gun Moll for Hire (S D Frances, December 1948). Art by Reginald Heade. (Image courtesy Steve Holland.)

No Regrets for Clara (S D Frances, March 1949). Art by Reginald Heade. (Image courtesy Steve Holland.)

Smart Girls Don't Talk (S D Frances, April 1949). Art by Reginald Heade. (Image courtesy Steve Holland.)

Smart Girls Don't Talk

By
HANK JANSON

Published by:-
S. D. FRANCES

Sole Distributors:
GAYWOOD PRESS LTD.,
30, GAYWOOD STREET, LONDON, S.E.1

The HANK JANSON Series

Smart Girls Don't Talk is the fifth in this series of Twelve stories by Tough-guy author, Hank Janson.

If you now want to follow his adventures across the States, ask your book-seller to reserve for you all future Hank Janson titles.

Next in this series to be published almost immediately

"LILLIES FOR MY LOVELY"
By
Hank Janson

Order your copy from your bookseller now to be sure of getting it.

OTHER BOOKS BY HANK JANSON

LADY, MIND THAT CORPSE

Sheila was disguised as a boy until another fella tried to strip away her pants. That started a rumpus which involved the important citizens of a town.

"What do you want me to do, Hank?" she asked quietly.

"Wait till I come back," I said. "And, lady, mind that corpse. Guard it with your life. Don't let anyone see it or I'll be in the jug, you'll be in the nut-house, Irwin will be in the chair, and Doone will have the laugh of his life."

This story will grip you from start to finish. We guarantee you will not put it down until the last page has been turned.

GUN MOLL FOR HIRE

It's a lousy set-up when your girl friend gets the eye from a dollar millionaire. And the set-up gets really complicated when the fella has a brother who is crazy, a sister-in-law who's made to strip-tease, a doctor who's a cardsharp and two tough henchmen who'll slit a throat at a dollar a time.

NO REGRETS FOR CLARA

When gangsters blow a bank and the heat is on, they're not inclined to stand on ceremony. Hi-jacking a launch, with its occupants, for a getaway is a bagatelle unless the occupants kick. And they did. But it was a loada grief all round, especially for the dames who got a beating. Even so, Clara learned a thing or two and that's why she had no regrets.

All these titles are available from your local bookseller at the popular price of 1s. 6d.

If you have difficulty in obtaining your copies, please write to the sole distributors:—

GAYWOOD PRESS, LTD.
30, GAYWOOD STREET, LONDON, S.E.1.

Top left: the title page for *Smart Girls Don't Talk*, in a layout typical of initial printings of the early first series novels.

Top right: the inside front covers of the books had by this stage started to feature promotional blurbs for the preceding titles.

Bottom left: while initial printings of the early first series novels generally had blank back covers, *Smart Girls Don't Talk* featured an advert for the forthcoming *Lilies for My Lovely*. (Note the misspelling of the first word of the latter title.)

Lilies for My Lovely (S D Frances, May 1949). Art by Reginald Heade. (Image courtesy Steve Holland.)

The very rare '12th Edition' of *Lilies for My Lovely* (New Fiction Press, 1953), with Reginald Heade art believed to have been intended originally for the 1951 novel *Milady Took the Rap*, but dropped at that time in favour of a plain graphic cover in an act of self-censorship, in the hope of avoiding trouble from the authorities; the white box in the top right-hand corner covers the original title.

Blonde on the Spot (S D Frances, June 1949). Art by Reginald Heade. (Image courtesy Steve Holland.)

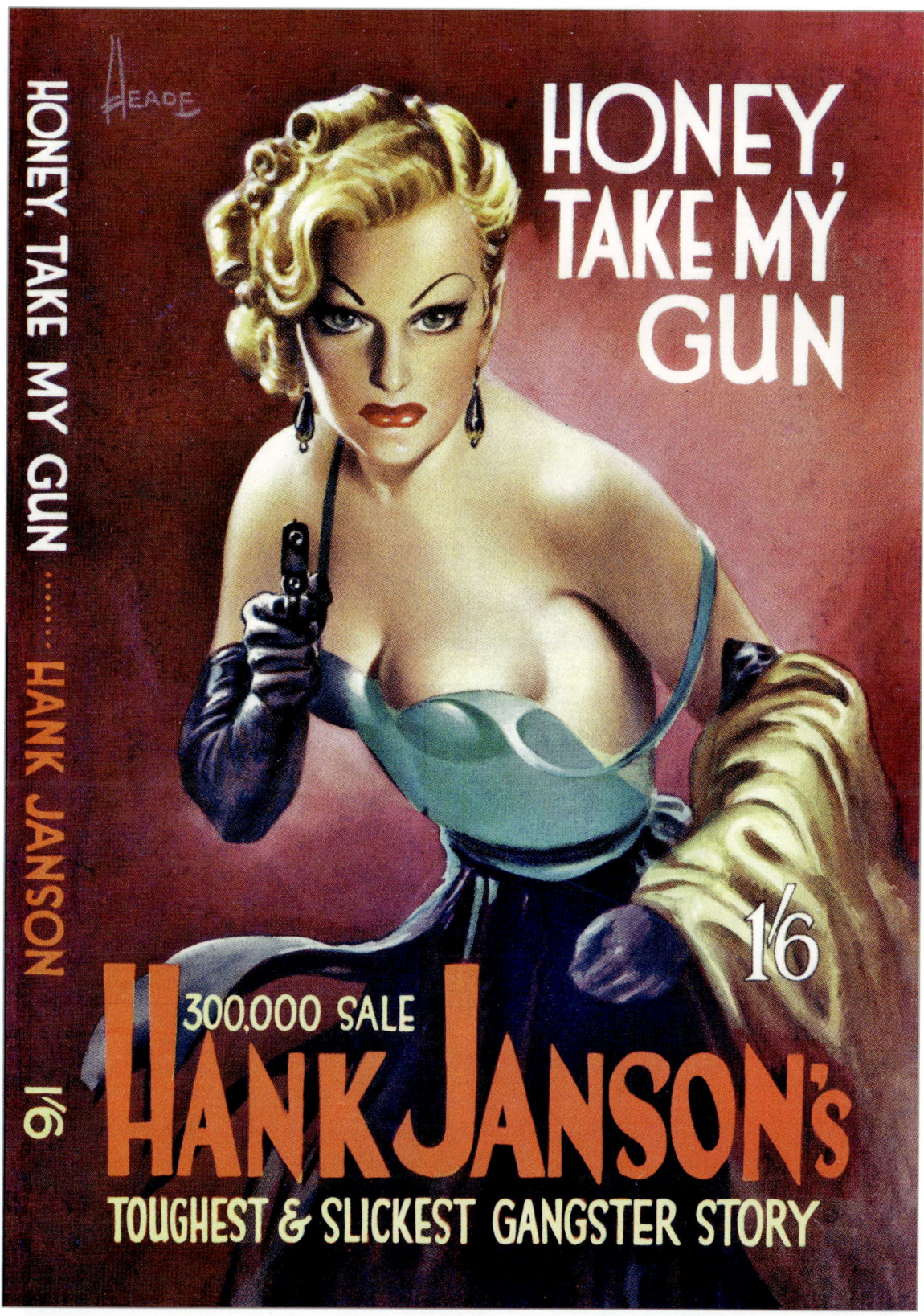

Honey, Take My Gun (S D Frances, July 1949). Art by Reginald Heade. (Image courtesy Steve Holland.)

Left: The rare '12th reprint' edition of *Blonde on the Spot* (Top Fiction Press, 1953), with Reginald Heade's art revised and given a much darker background, and his signature rendered almost invisible in the process.

Above: Stephen Frances pictured circa 1946, around the time when he created the Hank Janson character.

Below: Frances being interviewed in a Soho strip club, incognito as a masked Hank Janson.

Angel, Shoot to Kill (S D Frances, October 1949). Art by Reginald Heade.

The unused original cover for *Slay-Ride for Cutie* (S D Frances, November 1949). Art by Reginald Heade. (Image courtesy Steve Holland.)

The as-published cover for *Slay-Ride for Cutie* (S D Frances, November 1949). Art by Reginald Heade. (Image courtesy Steve Holland.)

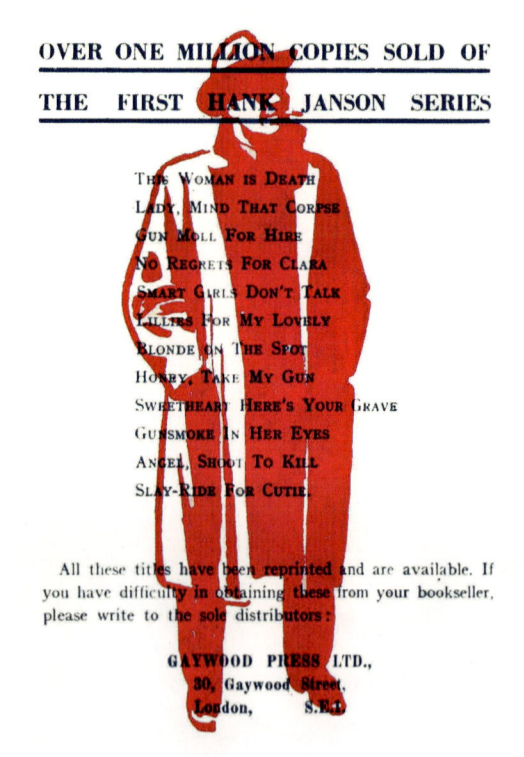

The new HANK JANSON series

As the present series of books by Hank Janson comes to an end, the publishers are carrying straight on with a completely fresh series.

This new series is based on the author's experiences while working as a reporter on a Chicago newspaper. There are twelve of these yarns and every one of them is written in the typical racy, tough, sexciting style that has earned Hank Janson the reputation of being one of to-day's best sellers.

The first of these stories will be:

"SISTER, DON'T HATE ME"

wherein Hank finds himself in a really tough spot, hiding from the police while handcuffed to a sweet-long-legged dame who is wanted for murder.

There were lots of angles that caused him grief, least important of which was being chained that way to a dame he didn't know. But even being chained to the dame was plenty exciting as you can figure for yourself. He just had to be around with her, whatever she did! And as dames go, adjusting a suspender is just a minor operation.

Hank Janson won't disappoint you one little bit with

"SISTER, DON'T HATE ME"

Top left: a standard titles listing printed on the back cover of first series reprints.

Bottom left: an advert for the debut second series novel, *Sister, Don't Hate Me*, printed at the back of *Slay-Ride for* Cutie.

Top right: the back cover of the first edition of *Sister, Don't Hate Me*.

Bottom right: *Sister, Don't Hate Me* had a typical second series title page, complete with Philip Mendoza-designed silhouette logo.

Sister, Don't Hate Me (S D Frances, December 1949). Art by Reginald Heade.

Some Look Better - Dead (S D Frances, January 1950). Art by Reginald Heade.

Sweetie, Hold Me Tight (S D Frances, February 1950). Art by Reginald Heade. (Image courtesy Steve Holland.)

Torment for Trixy (S D Frances, March 1950). Art by Reginald Heade. (Image courtesy Steve Holland.)

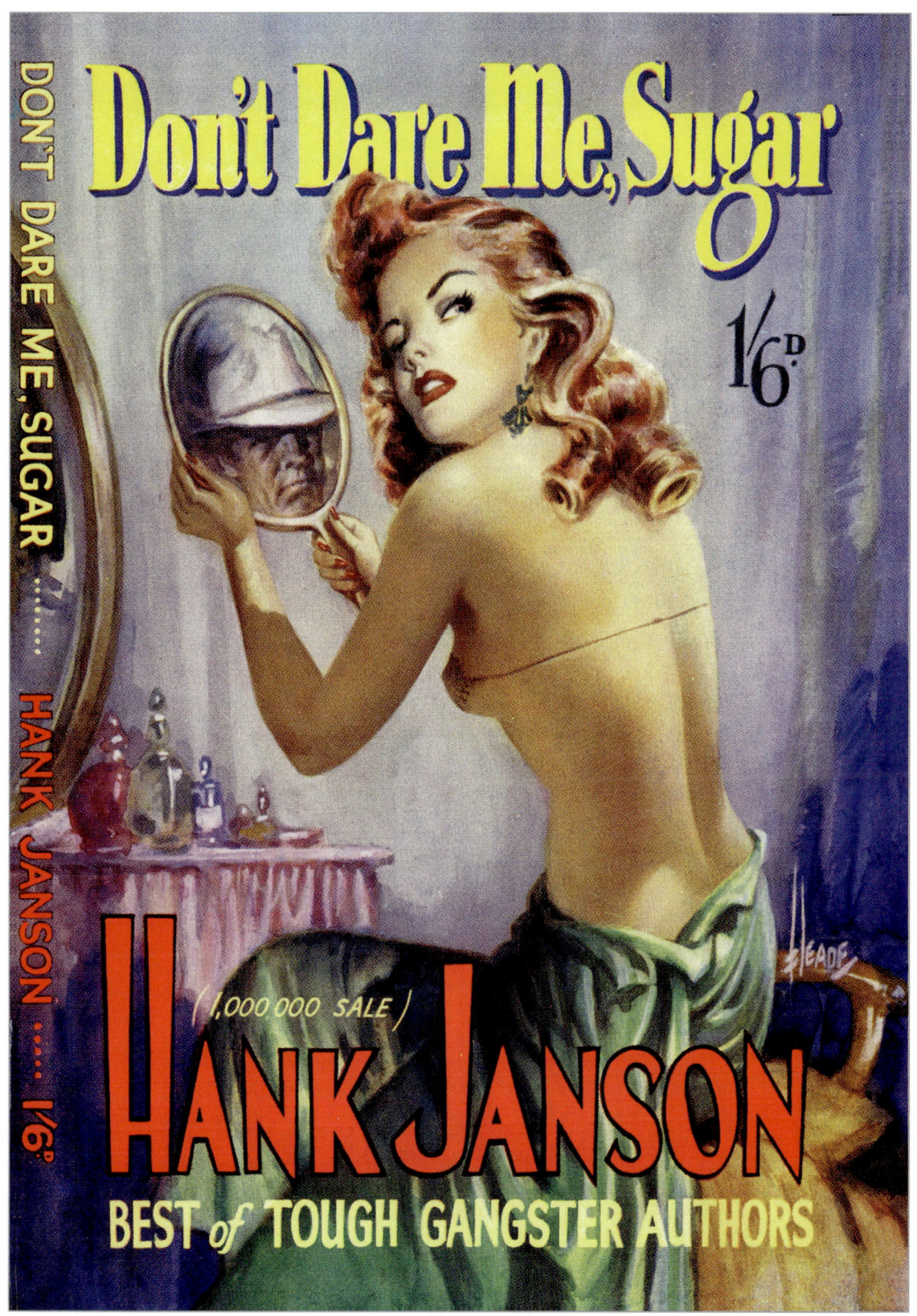

Don't Dare Me, Sugar (S D Frances, May 1950). Art by Reginald Heade. (Image courtesy Steve Holland.)

The Lady Has a Scar (S D Frances, June 1950). Art by Reginald Heade. (Image courtesy Steve Holland.)

The Jane With Green Eyes (S D Frances, July 1950). Art by Reginald Heade. (Image courtesy Steve Holland.)

Lola Brought Her Wreath (S D Frances, September 1950). Art by Reginald Heade. (Image courtesy Steve Holland.)

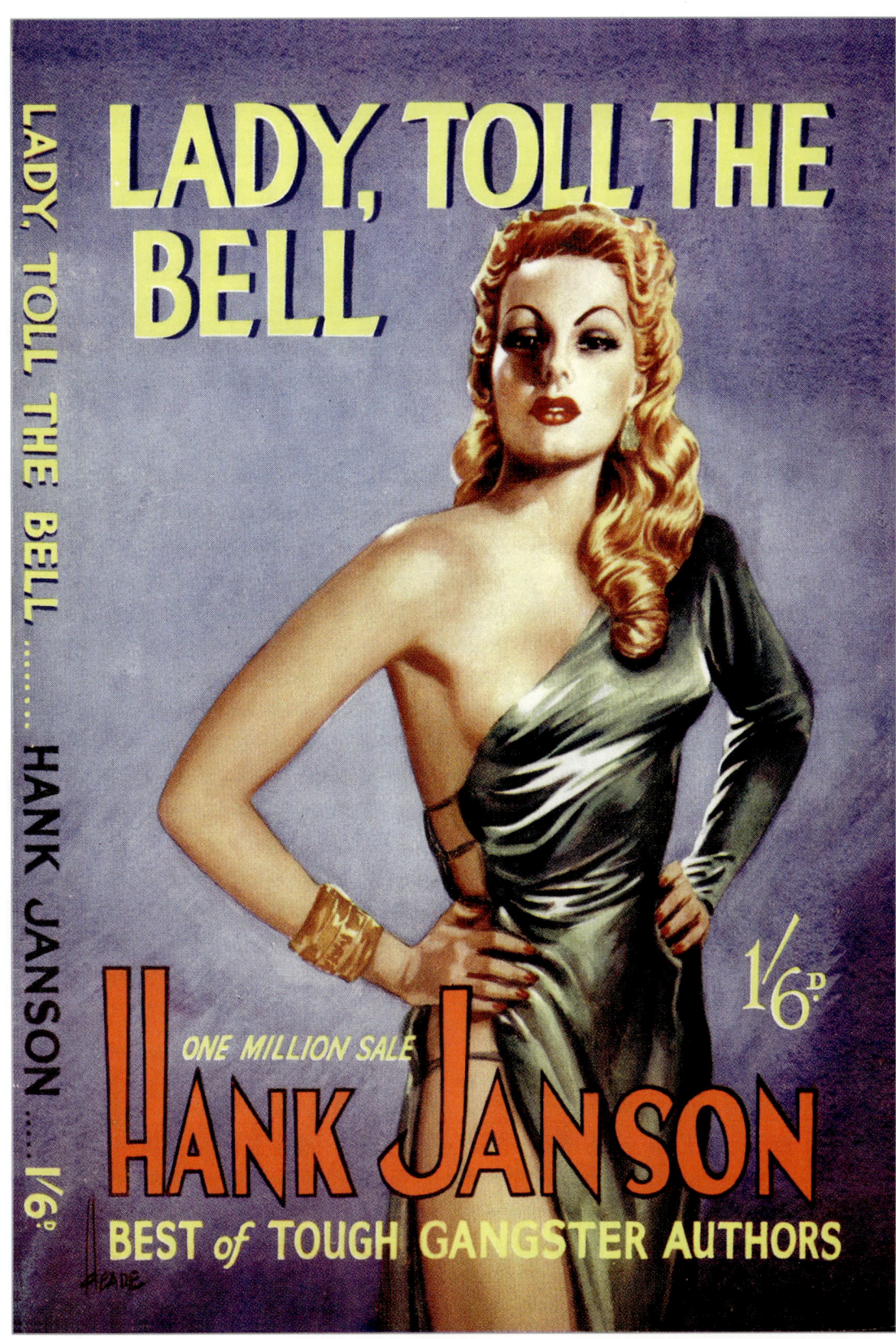

Lady, Toll the Bell (S D Frances, October 1950). Art by Reginald Heade. (Image courtesy Steve Holland.)

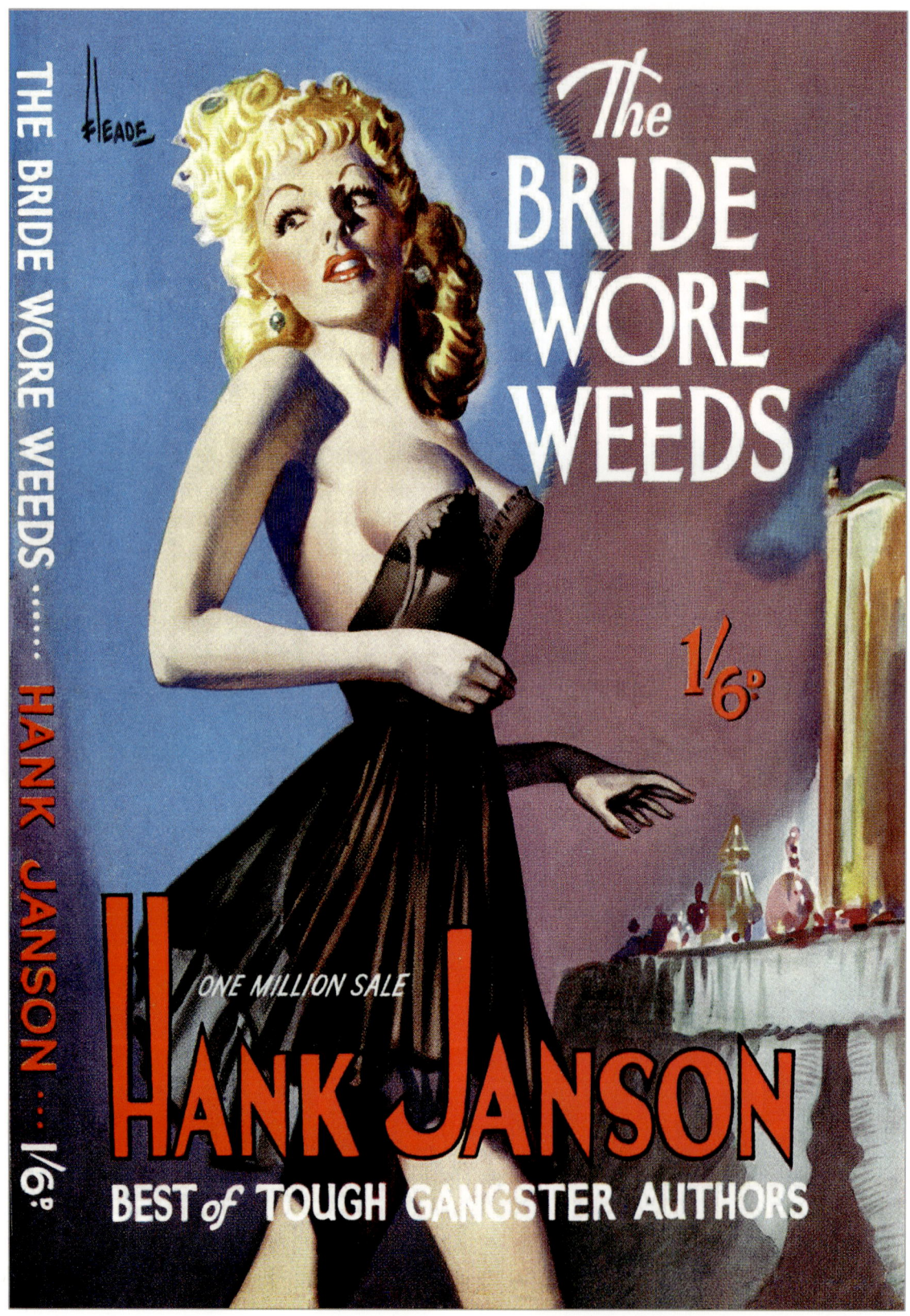

The Bride Wore Weeds (S D Frances, December 1950). Art by Reginald Heade. (Image courtesy Steve Holland.)

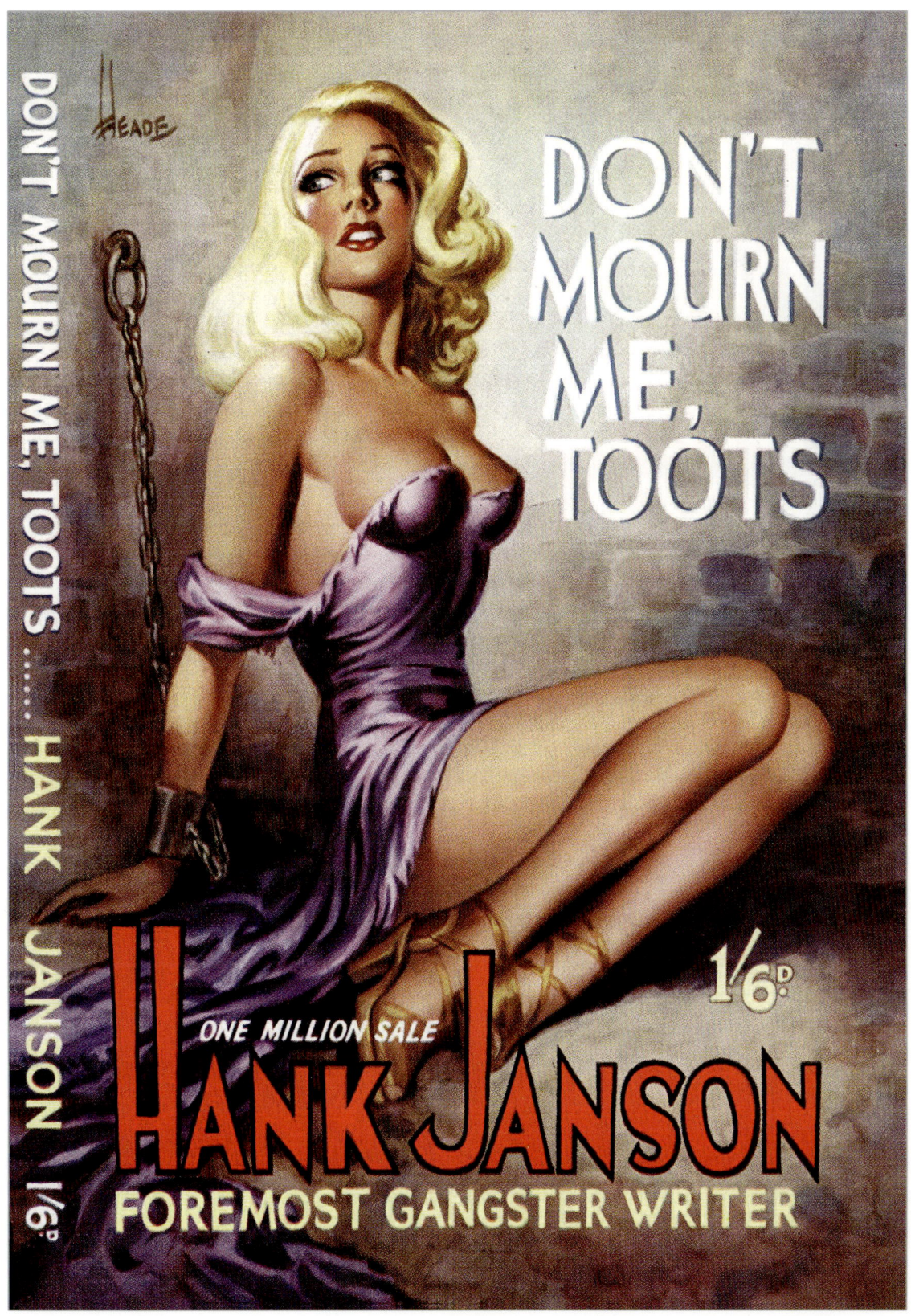

Don't Mourn Me, Toots (S D Frances, January 1951). Art by Reginald Heade. (Image courtesy Steve Holland.)

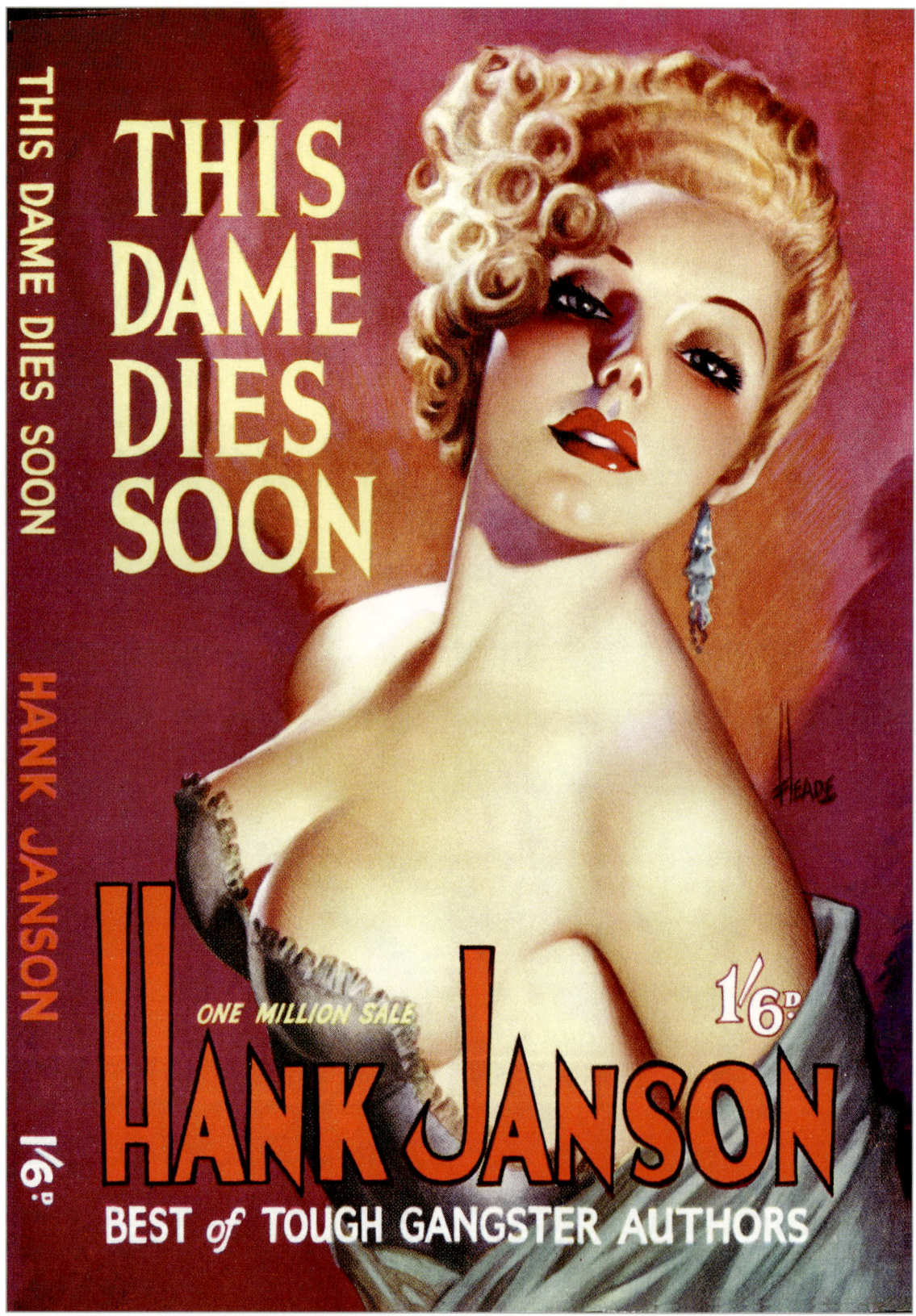

This Dame Dies Soon (S D Frances, February 1951). Art by Reginald Heade. (Image courtesy Steve Holland.)

THE CLASSIC ERA

OVER TWO MILLION COPIES SOLD OF THE FIRST HANK JANSON SERIES

This Woman is Death
Lady, Mind That Corpse
Gun Moll For Hire
No Regrets For Clara
Smart Girls Don't Talk
Lillies For My Lovely
Blonde on The Spot
Honey, Take My Gun
Sweetheart Here's Your Grave
Gunsmoke In Her Eyes
Angel, Shoot To Kill
Slay-Ride For Cutie

All these titles have been reprinted and are available. If you have difficulty in obtaining these from your bookseller, please write to the sole distributors:

GAYWOOD PRESS LTD.
30 GAYWOOD STREET
LONDON   S.E 1

THE THIRD HANK JANSON SERIES

This Dame Dies Soon is the last of the present series of twelve novels by Hank Janson.

The *Third Hank Janson Series* comprises twelve completely new novels, the first of which is entitled: *Baby Don't Dare Squeal*.

Readers will find these twelve new yarns contain all the suspense, drama and punch that characterizes each of Hank's books. We would like to quote the comments of a reader who sent us a letter of appreciation concerning our author:

"Every story is different, every line is packed with suspense and, once I begin to read, I find it impossible to lay the book down. But, best of all, is knowing from experience the next Hank Janson I read will be totally different from all the others, giving me a new and fresh pleasure."

We, the publishers, feel the same about Hank Janson's books. We believe and hope Hank Janson will go on giving pleasure to his readers in this way.

If you don't want to miss the First book of the New Series, ask your bookseller to reserve for you now:

"BABY, DON'T DARE SQUEAL"

THE HANK JANSON MAGAZINE

We have great pleasure in announcing to our readers, that starting early in 1951, we shall be publishing a new magazine entitled:

"UNDERWORLD"

This magazine will be Quarterly at first, because of the difficulty of paper supplies. As soon as possible it will be made into a monthly magazine.

Every issue will contain a full-length novelette by your favourite author Hank Janson. In addition, there will be selected short stories by other top ranking authors in this field of fiction.

The first issue will contain a long novelette entitled:

DOUBLE DOUBLE-CROSS
by HANK JANSON

THE MERRY WIDOW MURDER
by Ace Capelli

HONEYMOON WITH DEATH
by Dave Steel

EMILY WANTS TO KILL
by Max Clinten

BLACKMAIL
by Brad Shannon

Supplies of UNDERWORLD are likely to be severely rationed. We, therefore, earnestly urge our readers to ask their Booksellers to reserve copies of UNDERWORLD well in advance. Do not make the mistake of missing this thrill-packed magazine.

Top left: by the time the second series of Hank Janson novels ended in February 1951 with *This Dame Dies Soon*, the standard back-cover listing of the first series titles was boasting combined sales of over two million.

Top right: printed at the back of *This Dame Dies Soon* was this advert for the forthcoming third series of novels, beginning with *Baby, Don't Dare Squeal*.

Bottom left: printed for the first time at the back of the penultimate second series novel, *Don't Mourn Me, Toots*, was this advert for a new Stephen Frances venture: a Hank Janson magazine entitled *Underworld*. The same advert then appeared at the back of several third series novels as well. Although initially planned as a quarterly publication, increasing to monthly as soon as scarce post-war paper supplies allowed, *Underworld* eventually ran to just two issues, the first (see overleaf) appearing in 1951 and the second in 1952.

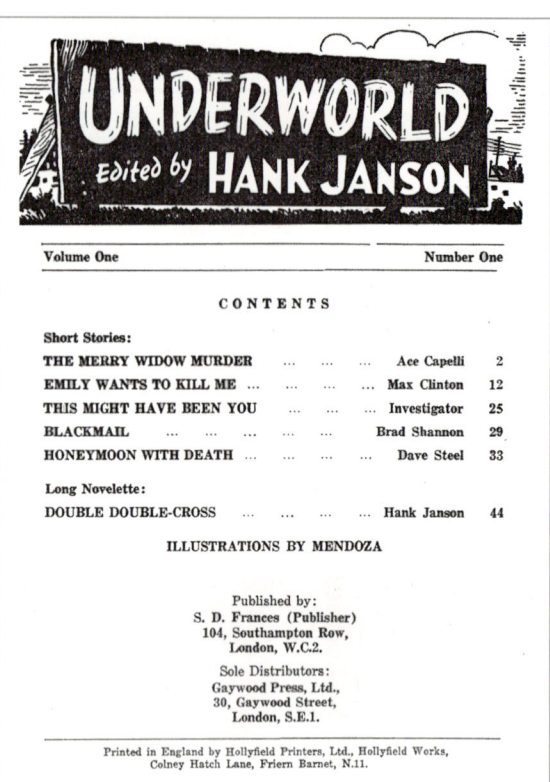

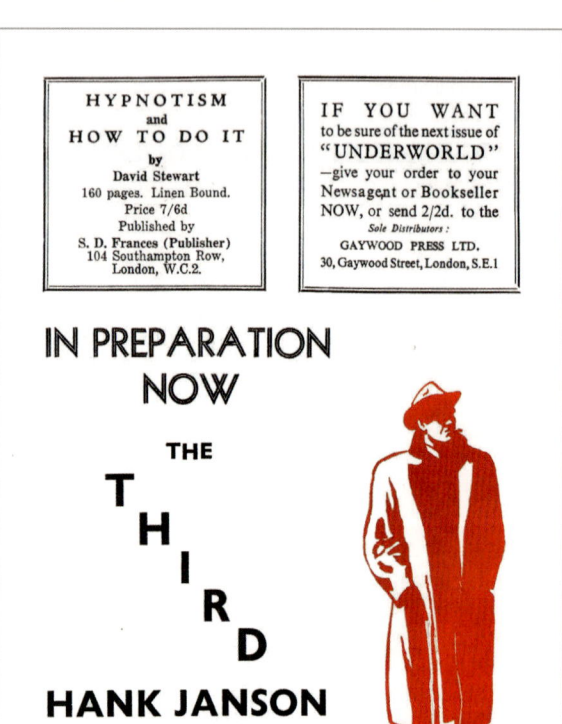

Top left: the front cover of the first issue of *Underworld* magazine (S D Frances, spring 1951)

Bottom left: the magazine's back cover.

Top right: the title page.

Centre right: Philip Mendoza's black-and-white title illustration for the magazine's Hank Janson short story, 'Double Double-Cross'.

THE CLASSIC ERA

This page: the other five Mendoza illustrations for the Hank Janson short story 'Double Double-Cross', featured in the first issue of *Underworld*.

Baby, Don't Dare Squeal (S D Frances, March 1951). Art by Reginald Heade. (Image courtesy Steve Holland.)

Death Wore a Petticoat (S D Frances, April 1951). Art by Reginald Heade. (Image courtesy Steve Holland.)

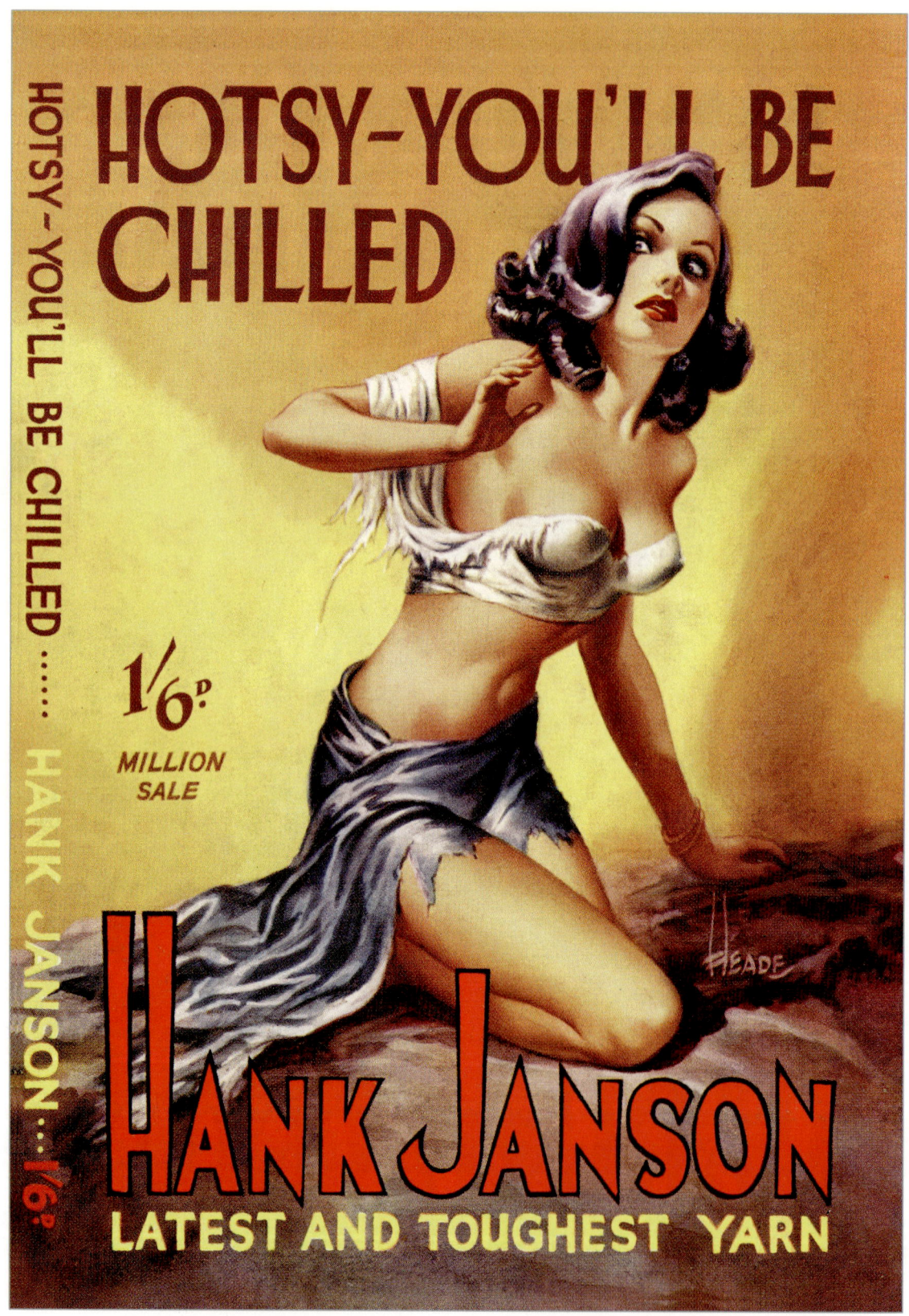

Hotsy – You'll Be Chilled (S D Frances, May 1951). Art by Reginald Heade. (Image courtesy Steve Holland.)

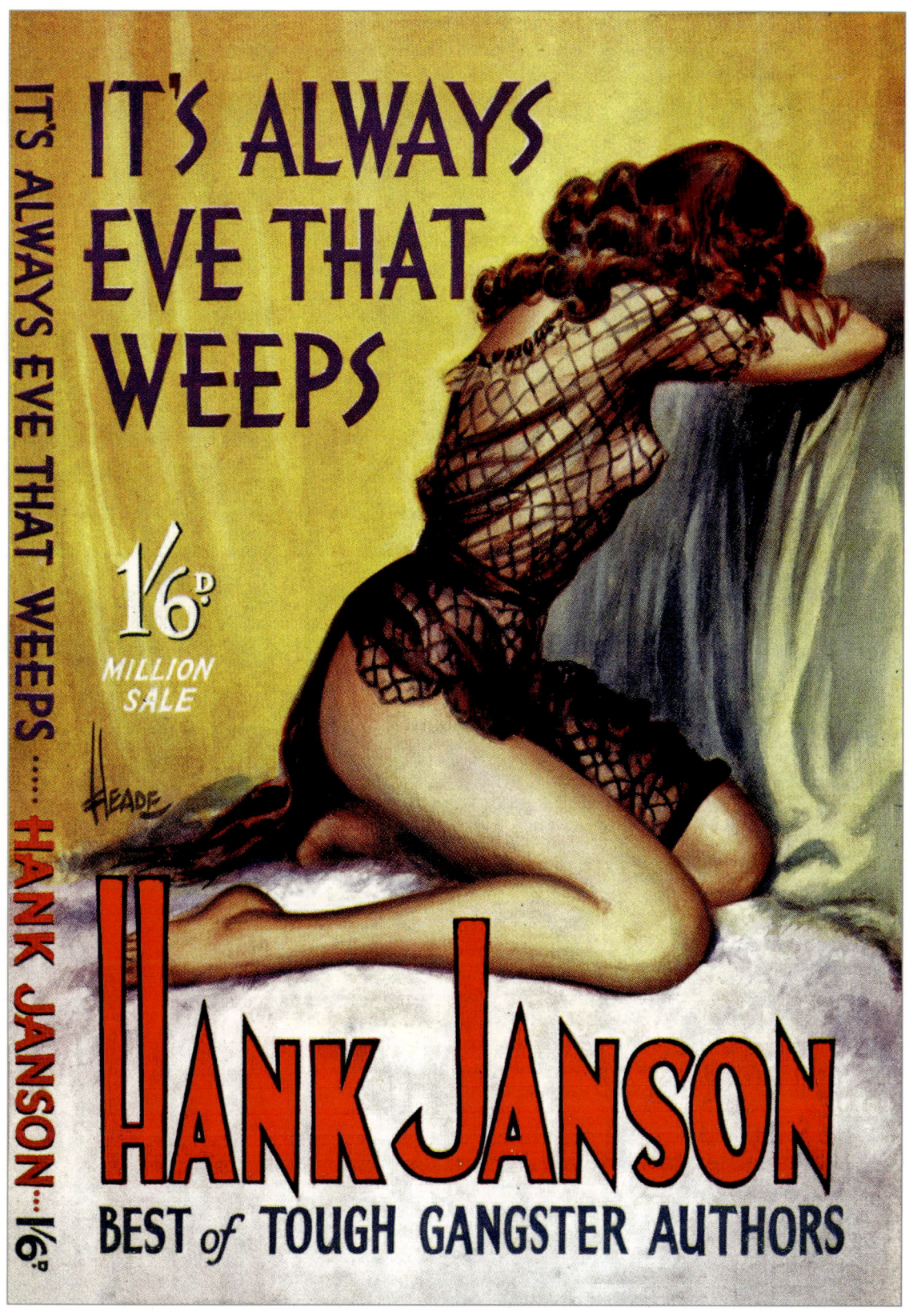
It's Always Eve That Weeps (S D Frances, June 1951). Art by Reginald Heade. (image courtesy Steve Holland.)

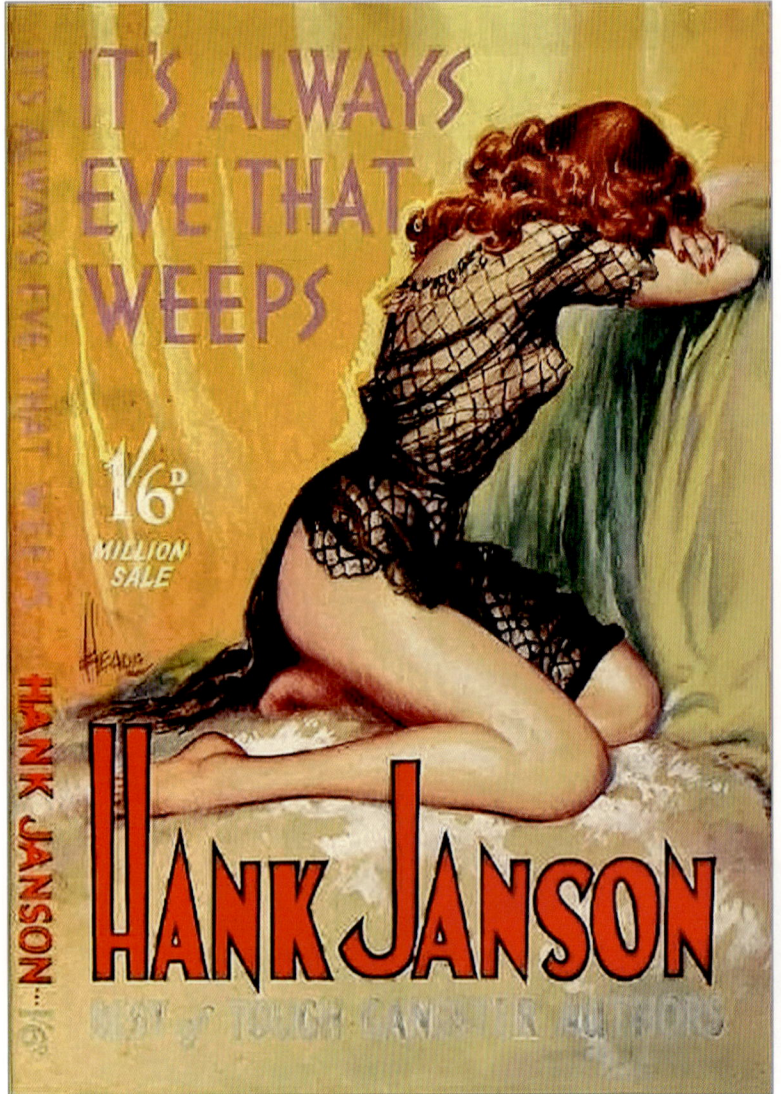
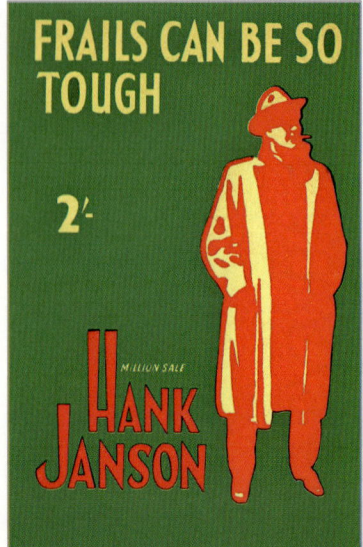

Above: Reginald Heade's original painting for *It's Always Eve That Weeps* (S D Frances, June 1951).

Top right: the as-published cover of *Frails Can Be So Tough* (New Fiction Press, August 1951). This was the first of a short run of covers where the originally-intended Reginald Heade art was dropped in favour of a graphic composition featuring the Hank Janson silhouette – a precaution taken in order to reduce the risk of copies of the books being seized and destroyed by the police or, worse still, giving rise to Obscene Publications Act prosecutions.

Centre right: Reginald Heade's original art for *Milady Took the Rap* (New Fiction Press, September 1951) is no longer known to exist, save for in repurposed form on the cover of the '12th Edition' of *Lilies for My Lovely* (see page 21); this is a reconstruction showing what it might have looked like.

Bottom right: the as-published cover of *Milady Took the Rap* (New Fiction Press, September 1951), with the colours and composition both essentially reversed from those of *Frails Can Be So Tough*.

Reginald Heade's original cover for *Frails Can Be So Tough* (New Fiction Press, August 1951). Although unused at the time, this was eventually reinstated for a Telos Publishing reissue in 2004. (Image courtesy Steve Holland.)

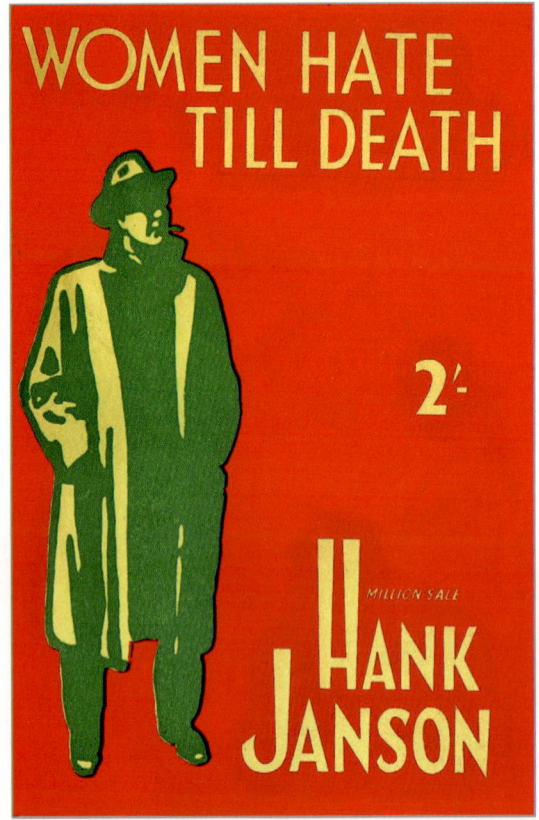

Top left: *Women Hate Till Death* (New Fiction Press, October 1951). No image is known to exist of the Reginald Heade art originally intended to grace this cover.

Bottom left: *Broads, Don't Scare Easy* (New Fiction Press, November 1951).

Bottom right: *Skirts Bring Me Sorrow* (New Fiction Press, November 1951).

These were the last of the Hank Janson first editions to appear with graphic silhouette covers. For the latter two, Reginald Heade artwork versions had already been printed, so these were 'silvered over' prior to publication, leaving only small sections of the artwork visible. Although many a schoolboy attempt was made to remove the silvering in order to discover what forbidden fruit lay beneath, this proved impossible. Heade's original art for *Broads, Don't Scare Easy* (see opposite) did however appear on a rare New Fiction Press reissue in December 1952; and his original art for *Skirts Bring Me Sorrow* (see page 54) eventually saw print many years later, on a Telos Publishing reissue of November 2003.

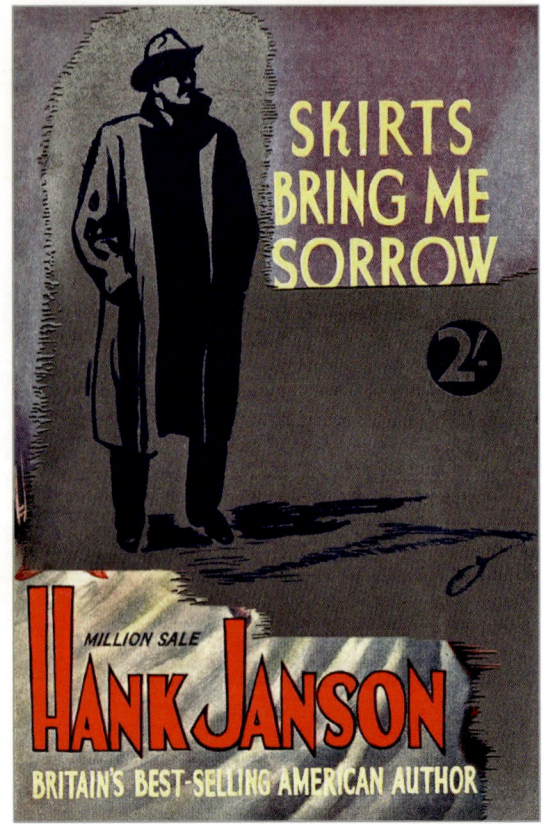

Reginald Heade's original cover for *Broads, Don't Scare Easy* (New Fiction Press, November 1951). (Image courtesy Steve Holland.)

Reginald Heade's original cover for *Skirts Bring Me Sorrow* (New Fiction Press, November 1951). (Image courtesy Steve Holland.)

Sadie, Don't Cry Now (New Fiction Press, January 1952). Art by Reginald Heade. (Image courtesy Steve Holland.)

Reginald Heade's painting for the cover originally intended to grace *Sadie, Don't Cry Now* (New Fiction Press, January 1952). This was dropped prior to publication in favour of the more chaste composition shown on the previous page. (Image courtesy Rian Hughes.)

THE CLASSIC ERA

The *Hank Janson* Magazine

YOU cannot afford to miss reading

Underworld

edited by HANK JANSON

Every issue contains a long novelette specially written for Underworld by Hank Janson

In addition, there are other stories by such well-known authors as Jack London, Brad Shannon, Damon Runyon, Max Clinten, Dave Steel, etc.

Supplies of UNDERWORLD are likely to be severely rationed. We, therefore, earnestly urge our readers to ask their Booksellers to reserve copies of UNDERWORLD well in advance. Do not make the mistake of missing this thrill-packed magazine

Left: Heade's original cover art for *Sadie, Don't Cry Now* was reinstated for a very rare New Fiction Press reissue published in 1953, with a darker green background substituted and a new price overlaid.

Above: a new advert for *Underworld*, printed at the back of the October 1951 title *Women Hate Till Death*. A second issue was then in preparation.

Below: throughout the third series, the books' back covers continued to present listings of the other available titles.

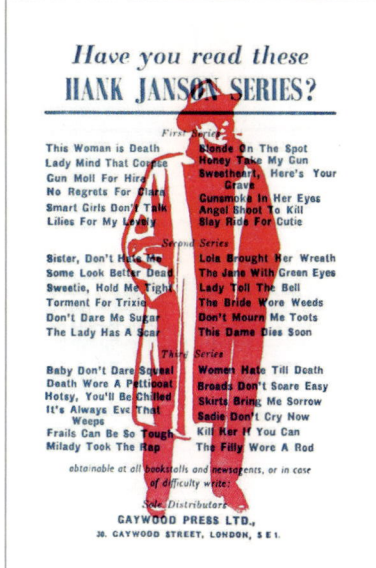

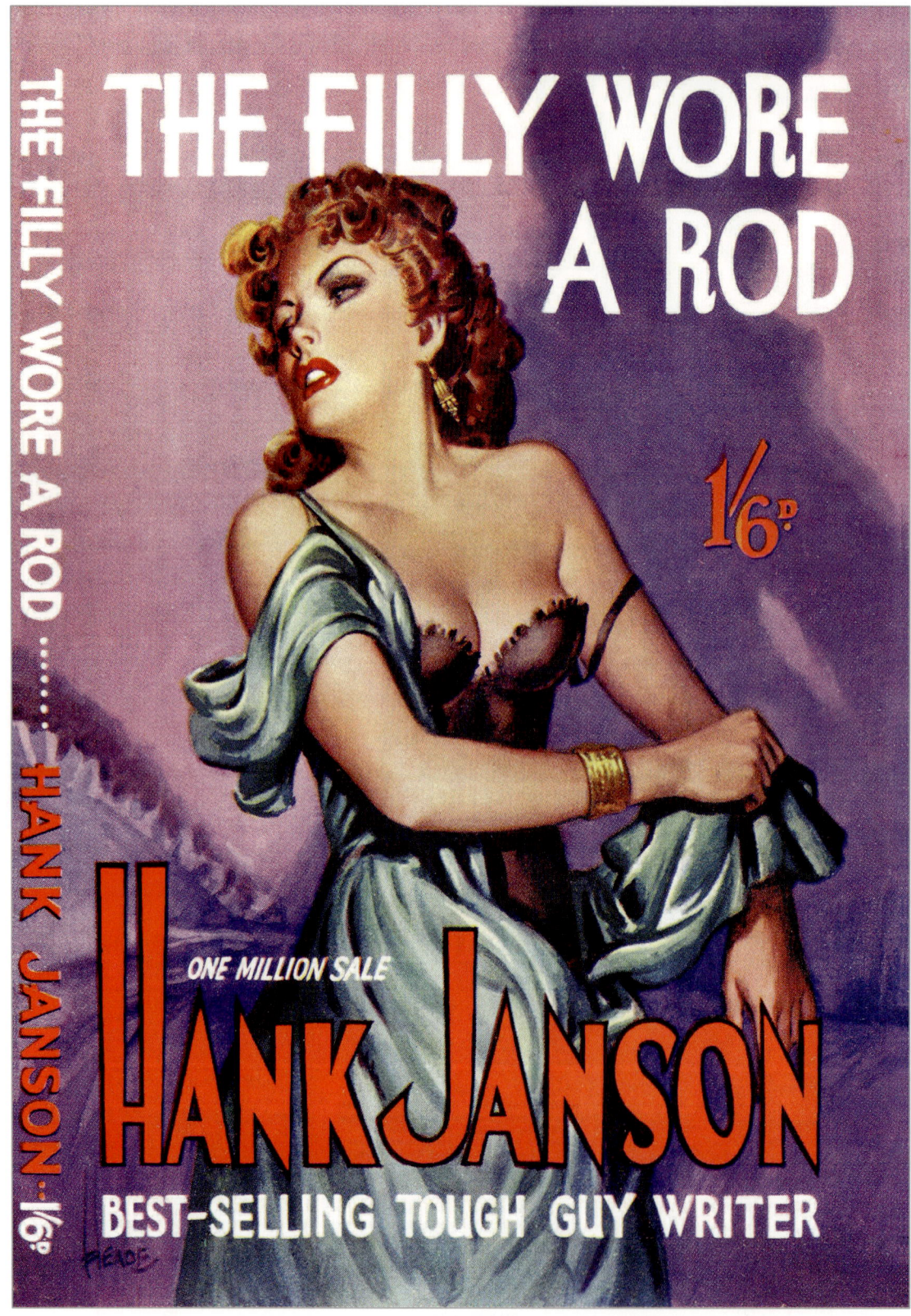

The Reginald Heade cover originally intended for *The Filly Wore a Rod* (New Fiction Press, February 1952). It was dropped prior to publication in favour of the more demure subject shown opposite. (Image courtesy Steve Holland.)

The as-published cover of *The Filly Wore a Rod* (New Fiction Press, February 1952). Art by Reginald Heade.

HANK JANSON UNDER COVER

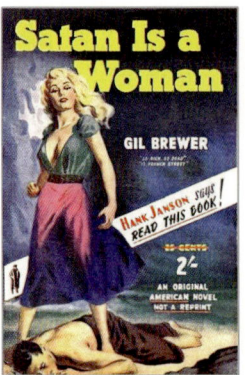

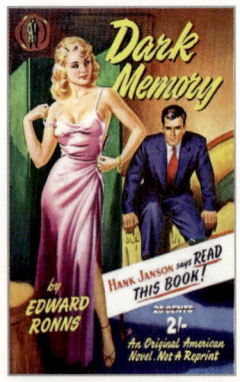

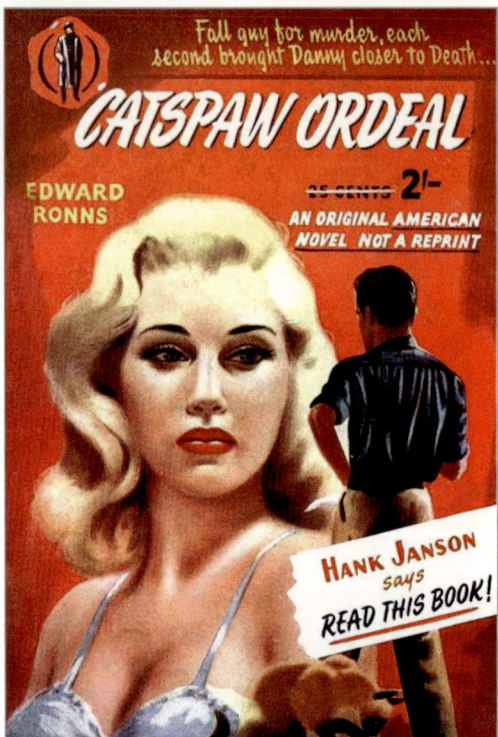

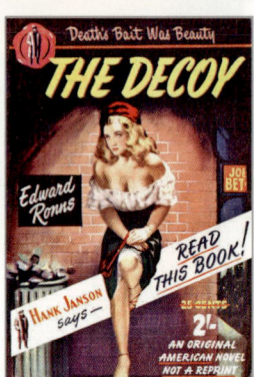
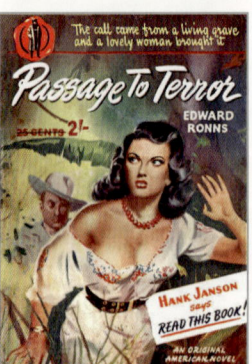
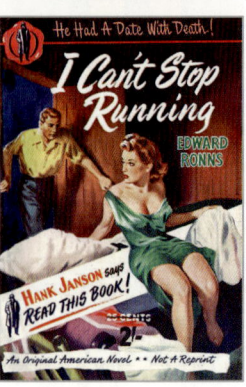

So popular had the Hank Janson novels become that in 1952 publishers New Fiction Press even started promoting their other crime titles with a front cover banner declaring 'Hank Janson says READ THIS BOOK!', in some cases accompanied in the top left-hand corner by a 'seal of approval' incorporating the familiar silhouette logo. Pictured above are ten examples. Listings of the Hank Janson titles also appeared on the backs of these books.

Kill Her If You Can (New Fiction Press, March 1952). Art by Reginald Heade. (Image courtesy Steve Holland.)

The new HANK JANSON Series

KILL HER IF YOU CAN is the last of the third series of **HANK JANSON** novels.

The sale of **HANK JANSON'S** books have been continually increasing month by month, proving beyond doubt that this author is surely one of the most prolific as well as one of the most widely read modern authors.

It gives us great pleasure, therefore, to inform our readers that **HANK JANSON** has contracted to write for us a fourth series of **HANK JANSON** novels; the first of which will be entitled:

MURDER

To make sure that you obtain a complete set of the fourth series, ask your bookseller now to reserve all future **HANK JANSON** titles that are published.

In case you should experience difficulty in obtaining your copies, write to the publishers:

NEW FICTION PRESS
79/80, CENTRAL BUILDINGS,
SOUTHWARK STREET,
LONDON, S.E.1.

Above: the title page of *Murder*.

Top left and below: adverts for the fourth series, printed at the back of *Kill Her If You Can* and *Murder* respectively.

Bottom left: also printed at the back of *Murder*, an advert for the first of a forthcoming series of irregular 'specials', which would be published alongside the standard novels.

SPECIAL ANNOUNCEMENT !

During the last few months **HANK JANSON** has spent much of his spare time preparing and writing a book that is quite distinct and quite different to any book he has written in the **HANK JANSON** series.

We, the publishers, have read this book and without hesitation have placed it in hand for production and publication at the earliest possible moment.

We have not the slightest doubt that every reader of **HANK JANSON** will want to read this dynamic, stirring and satisfying **HANK JANSON "SPECIAL."**

AUCTIONED

A story of mysterious and exciting Persia, a beautiful girl sold into slavery, publicly auctioned in the market-place, and purchased for a Sultan's concubine.

In the powerful descriptive style that has endeared Hank Janson to his readers, the author paints vivid word pictures of Eastern customs, the fears, experiences and punishments endured by female slaves in the seclusion of the Harem, the harsh brutality of rulers who are all powerful and of the man who dared a Sultan's vengeance.

★ THIS IS A HANK JANSON SPECIAL ★
★★ SUPPLIES WILL BE LIMITED, SO ORDER ★★
FROM YOUR BOOKSELLER NOW TO AVOID DISAPPOINTMENT
★★★ READY AND ON SALE VERY SHORTLY AT ★★★
THE USUAL PRICE OF 2/-

Don't Miss
"AUCTIONED" The Hank Janson **"SPECIAL"**

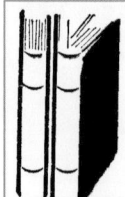

The new HANK JANSON Series

MURDER is the first of the fourth series of **HANK JANSON** novels.

The sale of **HANK JANSON'S** books have been continually increasing month by month, proving beyond doubt that this author is surely one of the most prolific as well as one of the most widely read modern authors.

To make sure you obtain a complete set of the fourth series, ask your bookseller **NOW** to reserve all future **HANK JANSON** titles that are published. The next title in this series, ready shortly is **TENSION**.

NEW FICTION PRESS
79/80, CENTRAL BUILDINGS,
SOUTHWARK STREET,
LONDON, S.E.1.

Murder (New Fiction Press, April 1952). Art by Reginald Heade. (Image courtesy Steve Holland.)

Conflict (New Fiction Press, June 1952). Art by Reginald Heade. (Image courtesy Steve Holland.)

Auctioned (New Fiction Press, June 1952), the first of the new 'specials'. Art by Reginald Heade. (Image courtesy Steve Holland.)

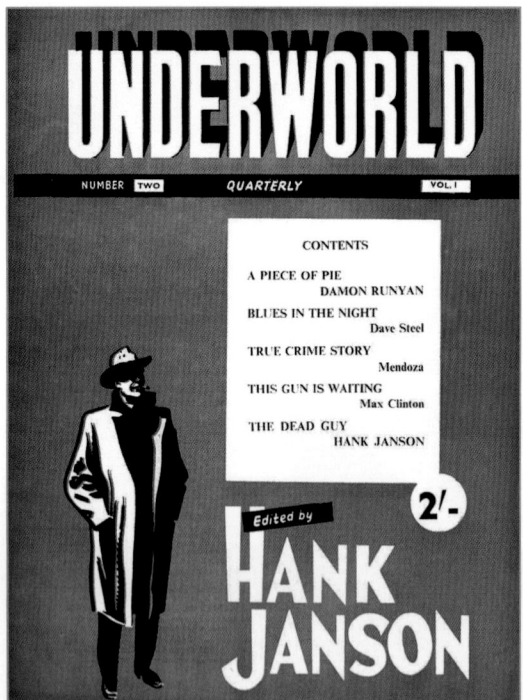
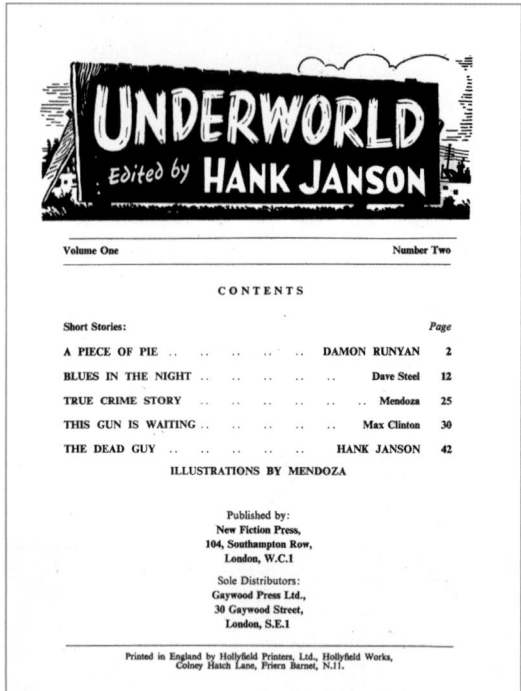

Top left: the front cover of the second issue of *Underworld* (New Fiction Press, spring 1952). Top right: the magazine's title page. Bottom: Mendoza's title illustration for the Hank Janson story 'The Dead Guy' – unusually, including a depiction of Janson himself.

THE CLASSIC ERA

Left and above: Mendoza's other two illustrations for the *Underworld* short story 'The Dead Guy'.

Below: a notice that appeared on the magazine's inside front cover.

HANK JANSON

We are pleased to inform readers of Hank Janson that we have been able to issue a limited number of reprints of Hank Janson's earlier books which hitherto were unobtainable.

Among these reprints being issued are :

The Bride Wore Weeds; Slay-ride for Cutie; Death Wore a Petticoat; Broads Don't Scare Easy; Angel Shoot to Kill; Frails Can be so Tough; Lady Toll The Bell; Baby Don't Dare Squeal; This Dame Dies Soon; Don't Dare me Sugar; Sweetheart Here's Your Grave; and *Gunsmoke In Her Eyes.*

Ask your bookseller now to order any titles you need to complete your collection while these titles are still available.

Tension (New Fiction Press, July 1952). Art by Reginald Heade.

Whiplash (New Fiction Press, August 1952). Art by Reginald Heade. (Image courtesy Steve Holland.)

Accused (New Fiction Press, October 1952). Art by Reginald Heade. (Image courtesy Steve Holland.)

Killer (New Fiction Press, November 1952). Art by Reginald Heade.

The second 'special', *Persian Pride* (New Fiction Press, November 1952). Often attributed to Heade, this cover was actually by a different artist, identity unknown, imitating his style; the woman's body was copied from Heade's *Auctioned* painting (see page 65).

Suspense (New Fiction Press, December 1952). Art by Reginald Heade. (Image courtesy Steve Holland.)

Pursuit (New Fiction Press, January 1953). Art by Reginald Heade.

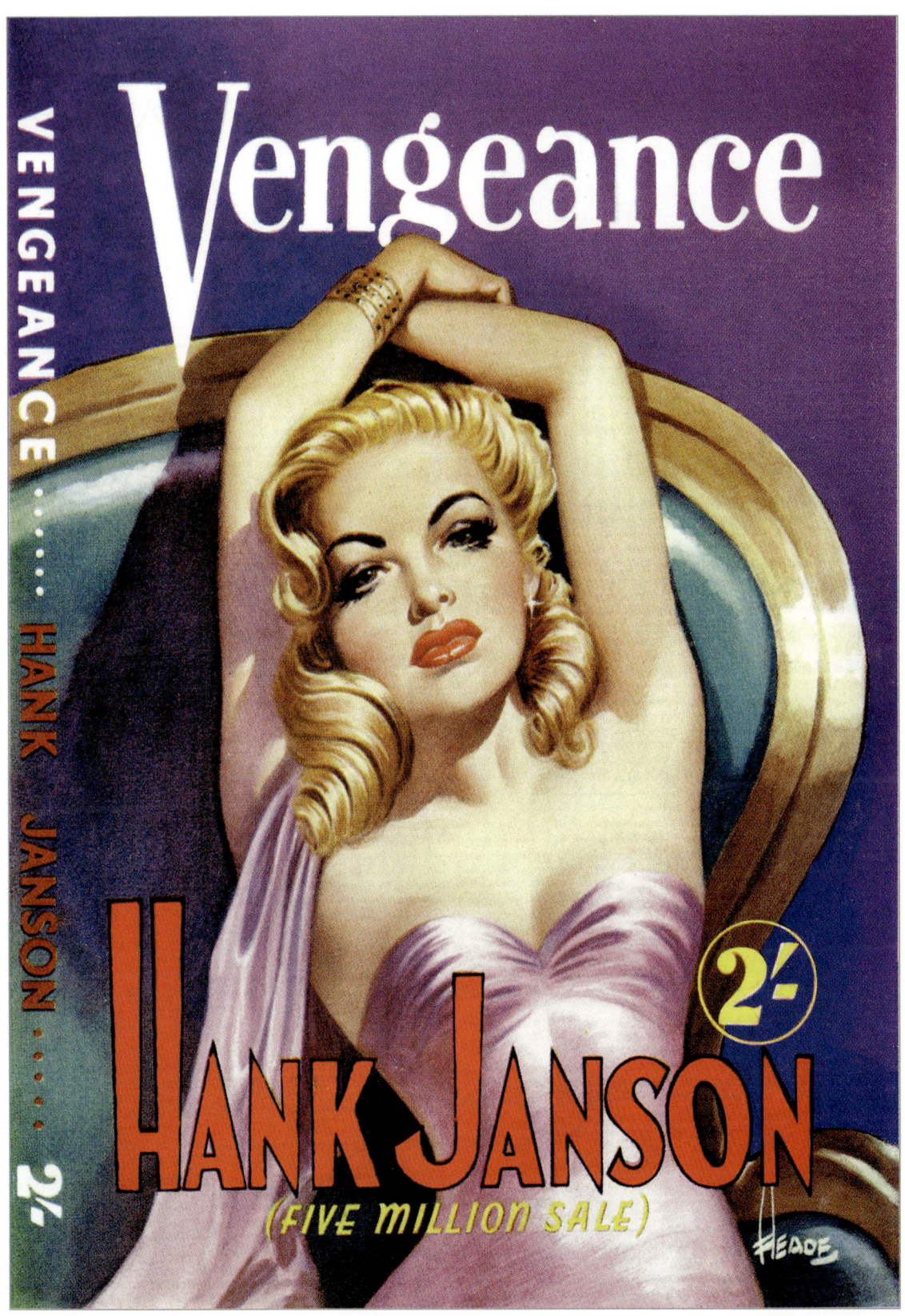

Vengeance (New Fiction Press, February 1953). Art by Reginald Heade. (Image courtesy Steve Holland.)

Above: the front cover and title page of *Britain's Great Flood Disaster* (New Fiction Press, March 1953) — a very different type of Hank Janson book. Stephen Frances and publisher Reginald Carter devised this charitable project — a large-format, soft-covered, 64-page glossy publication full of black-and-white photographs — in order to raise money for the victims of extensive flooding suffered along England's east coast after a severe storm struck on 31 January 1953.

Below left: an advert for *Britain's Great Flood Disaster*, printed at the back of the Hank Janson novel *Torment*.

Below right: the familiar back-cover titles listing had by this time been expanded to include the recently-published novels.

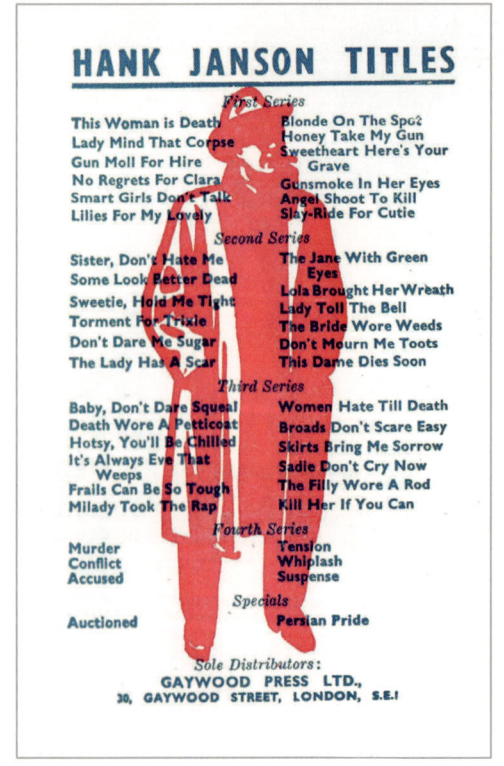

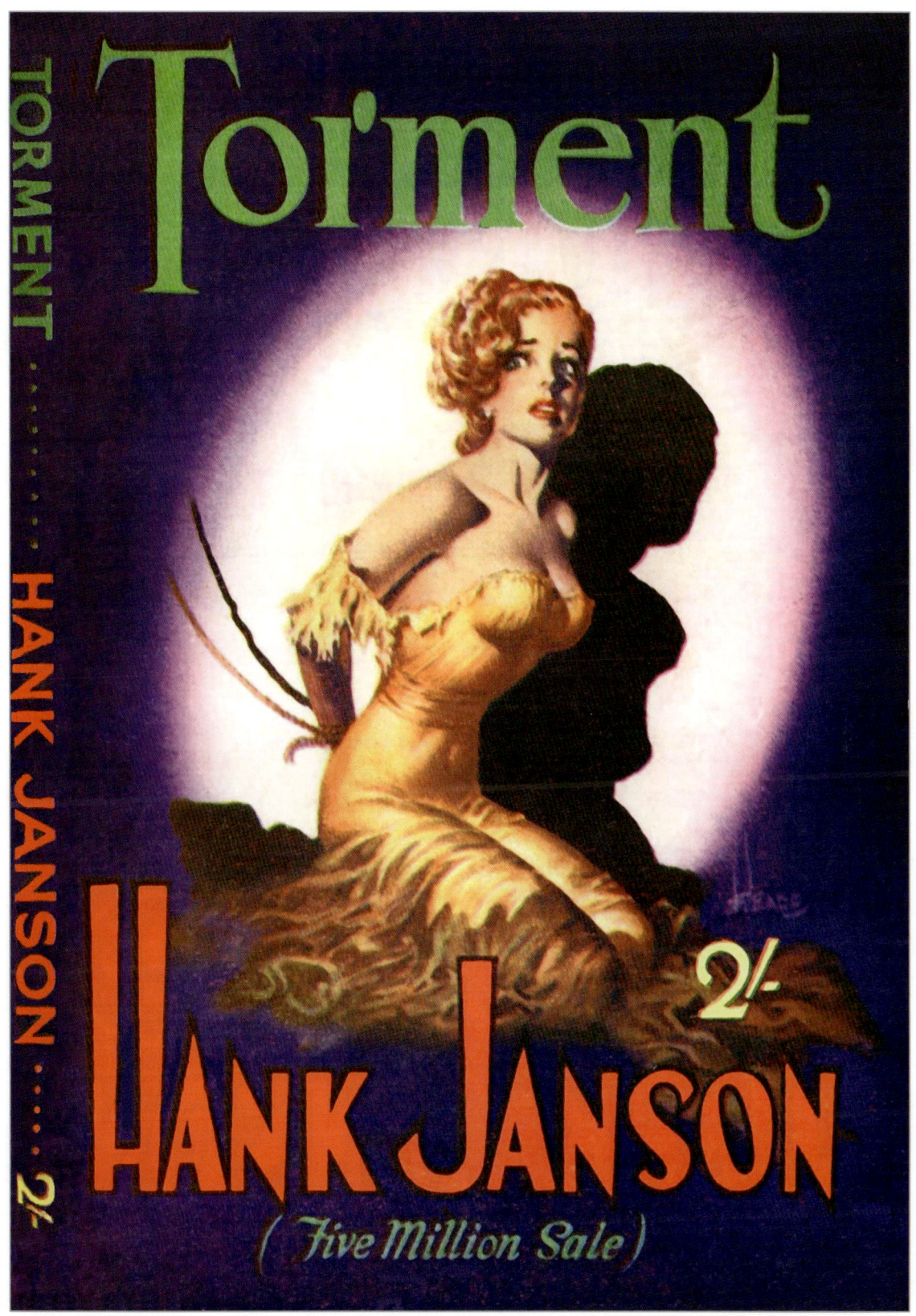

Torment (New Fiction Press, April 1953). Art by Reginald Heade.

Amok (New Fiction Press, May 1953). Art by Reginald Heade.

The final fourth series novel, *Corruption* (Top Fiction Press, June 1953). Art by Reginald Heade.

Above: printed at the back of several of the fourth series novels were adverts for some of the other New Fiction Press crime titles 'recommended' by Hank Janson (see page 60). Although promoted by the publishers as being by Gil Brewer, *I, Mobster* was in fact written anonymously by Joseph Hilton Smyth; similarly, although listed in these adverts as an Edward Ronns novel, *The Lady Kills* was actually the work of, and credited in the book itself to, Bruno Fischer.

Below: adverts for the song 'Hank Janson Blues', sung by Anne Shelton (see opposite). These appeared on the inside front and back covers of a number of the Janson novels, starting with *Amok*. (Unlike in these adverts, the song title actually had no initial 'The'.)

Such was the popularity of the Hank Janson books that in 1953 they even spawned a novelty pop single, 'Hank Janson Blues', by English vocalist Anne Shelton. The Peter Cornish-written track received no BBC radio play, as they considered it breached their rule forbidding advertising. The sheet music was published by New Fiction Press, also in 1953, with Reginald Heade cover art (above).

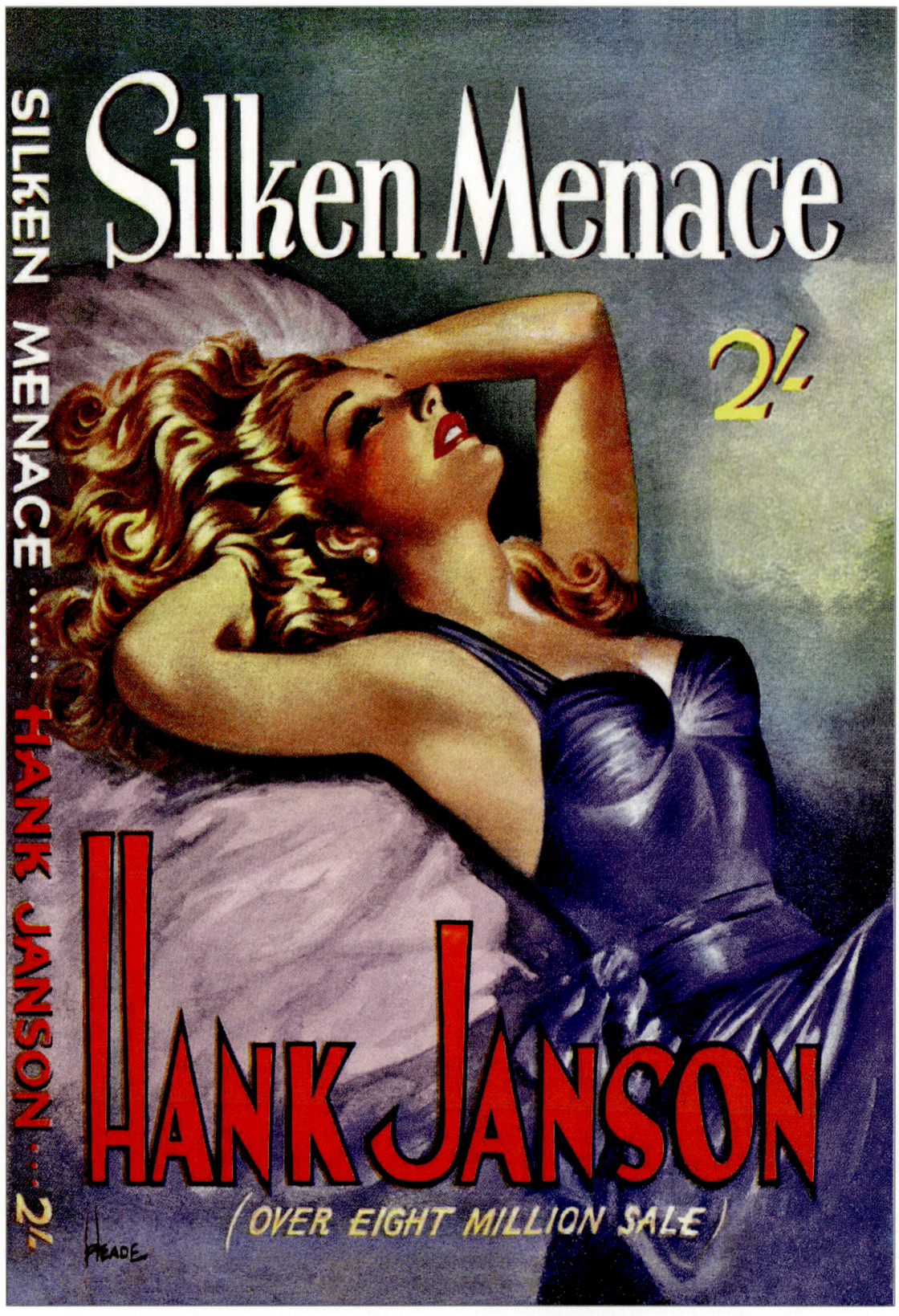

The first fifth series novel, *Silken Menace* (Top Fiction Press, July 1953). Art by Reginald Heade. (Image courtesy Steve Holland.)

The third of the 'specials' – completing a Persian trilogy – *Desert Fury* (New Fiction Press, July 1953). Art by Reginald Heade.

Nyloned Avenger (Top Fiction Press, August 1953). Art by Reginald Heade. (Image courtesy Steve Holland.)

THE CLASSIC ERA

The fourth of the 'specials', *The Unseen Assassin* (Top Fiction Press, August 1953). Foreground figure by Reginald Heade, background by Ron Turner. This unusual foray into the science-fiction genre had been promoted at the back of *Corruption* and *Desert Fury* by way of a six-page 'personal letter' from Hank to his readers. *The Unseen Assassin* itself closed with another, shorter letter, in which Hank offered a £20 prize to the reader who wrote in with the most perceptive feedback on the book. (Image courtesy Steve Holland.)

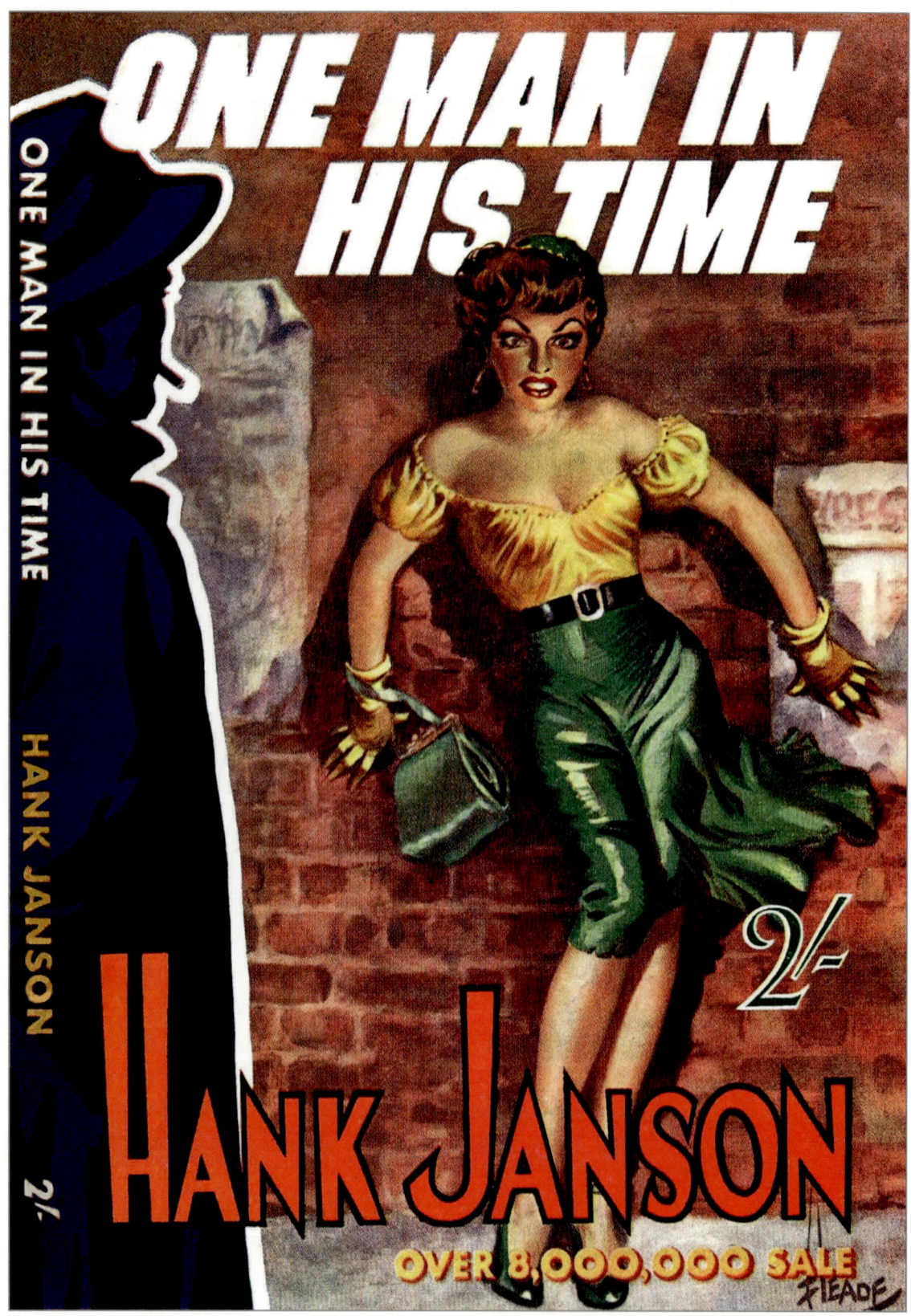

The fifth 'special', *One Man In His Time* (New Fiction Press, August 1953). Art by Reginald Heade.

THE CLASSIC ERA

A very Special
SPECIAL
by
HANK JANSON

Hank Janson is one of the most prolific writers as well as the best-selling author in his line. In the past four years he has written more than fifty books all of which have been reprinted and re-issued a great many times.

Therefore, when our author deliberately slashes what little leisure time he has to write a "Special," the readers know this book is exceptional.

A "Special" is a book Hank Janson is burning to write and "ONE MAN IN HIS TIME" is red-hot, alive and dynamic, pulsing with excitement and suspense.—In a phrase it's "Hank Janson at his best."

"ONE MAN IN HIS TIME," in the opinion of our advisers, is, indeed, Hank Janson at his best. "The best he has ever written," are the reports given to us.

We seriously advise our readers therefore to order from their booksellers NOW "One Man In His Time" which will be ready very soon. It will prove the most unusual, thrilling and gripping book you have ever read.

READY AUGUST   144 Pages.   2/-.

Obtainable from
GAYWOOD PRESS LIMITED
30, GAYWOOD STREET, LONDON, S.E.1

FOREWORD

Hank JANSON, reporter on a Chicago newspaper, has concluded a series of novels dealing with his experiences as a newspaper reporter.

This present new series of novels is based on Hank Janson's experiences while taking an enforced vacation on the Continent with nothing to worry him other than a burning curiosity and an unerring ability to involve himself in all kinds of difficulties.

SILKEN MENACE is the first novel of the fifth "Continental" series.

The publishers have pleasure in announcing that Hank Janson has now concluded for us a *Fifth Series* of his novels.

The author now writes about his experiences on the Continent, travelling from one country to another, meeting all kinds of difficulties, enduring many hardships and encountering more than his full share of thrills.

Those readers of Hank Janson who have read his books faithfully for many years will know they can count on the same rich, suspenseful narrative that has made Hank Janson one of their most popular authors.

The first book in this series is SILKEN MENACE, to be followed almost immediately by NYLONED AVENGER.

We earnestly suggest to our readers that to make sure of receiving their copy they should place an order with their bookseller at the earliest possible moment.

Should any difficulty be experienced in obtaining copies, please write direct to the distributors:

GAYWOOD PRESS LTD.
30 GAYWOOD STREET, LONDON, S.E.1

ONE MAN IN HIS TIME

BY
HANK JANSON

Published by
NEW FICTION PRESS LTD.
139, Borough High Street, S.E.1

Sole Distributors:
GAYWOOD PRESS LTD., 30, GAYWOOD ST., LONDON, S.E.1

Top left: the closing pages of the third 'special', *Desert Fury*, promoted not only the fourth, *The Unseen Assassin*, with a repeat of the 'personal letter' from Hank Janson first printed at the end of *Corruption*, but also the fifth, *One Man In His Time*, by way of this advert. Described here as a book Hank Janson was 'burning to write', *One Man In His Time* was actually a reissue of a semi-autobiographical novel that Stephen Frances had first issued under his own name as a now-scarce Pendulum Publications hardback in 1946.

Bottom left: the title page of *One Man In His Time*, including the revised version of the silhouette logo that first started to appear toward the end of the fourth series of novels.

Above: the debut fifth series novel, *Silken Menace*, included both a foreword (top) and a closing note (bottom) explaining this series' new 'Continental' premise, which would see Hank leaving behind his job as *Chicago Chronicle*'s ace crime reporter and instead having adventures in various countries around Europe. Although this series was planned to run, like the previous four, to 12 titles in total, in the end only *Silken Menace* and *Nyloned Avenger* were published, bringing the classic-era Hank Janson range to an end.

Woman Trap (Top Fiction Press, unpublished, intended for September 1953). Art by Reginald Heade. (Image courtesy Steve Holland.)

Perfumed Nemesis (Top Fiction Press, unpublished, intended for October 1953). Art by Reginald Heade. (Image courtesy Steve Holland.)

Blonde Dupe (Top Fiction Press, unpublished, intended for November 1953). Art by Reginald Heade. (Image courtesy Steve Holland.)

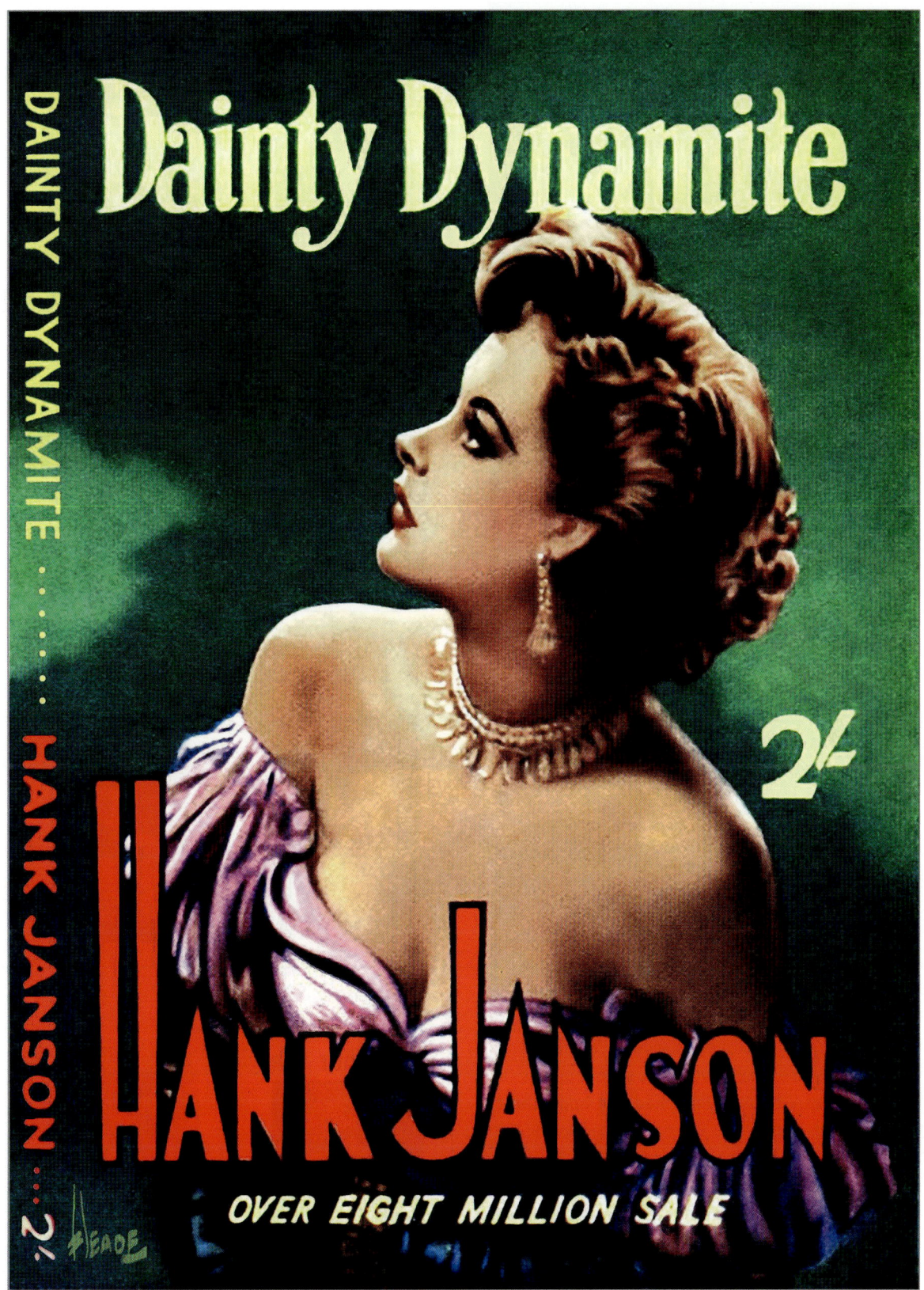

Dainty Dynamite (Top Fiction Press, unpublished, intended for December 1953). Art by Reginald Heade.

HANK JANSON UNDER COVER

Above: Reginald Heade's cover for the anthology *Deadly Mission* (Top Fiction Press, 1953). (Image courtesy Steve Holland.)

Top Fiction Press was the new imprint that publisher Reginald Carter set up to continue the Hank Janson range after his previous New Fiction Press was bankrupted by Obscene Publications Act prosecutions. *Corruption*, *Silken Menace*, *Nyloned Avenger* and *The Unseen Assassin* are the only titles known for certain to have appeared under the new name, overlapping in July and August 1953 with the last of those under the old one, as Carter rushed to clear that existing stock. *Deadly Mission* was also planned as a Top Fiction book, but it is uncertain if it was actually published; a couple of copies do exist, but these may have been simply proofs. Its three stories – two of which had first appeared in *Underworld* magazine – were reprinted in 1958 in the Alexander Moring-published *Kill This Man*. The *Deadly Mission* title was also reused by Stephen Frances in the Moring era, for a 1955 Janson novel.

Right: toward the end of the fourth series, the back covers of the novels began to present, in place of titles listings, simple monochrome or, more usually, full colour adverts for forthcoming titles. Pictured here are eight examples.

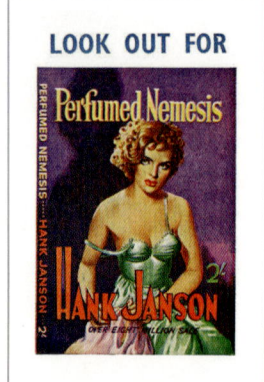
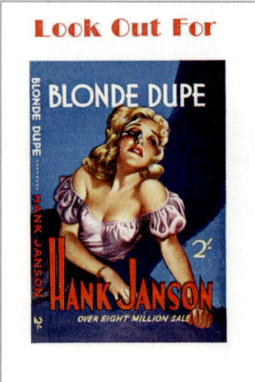
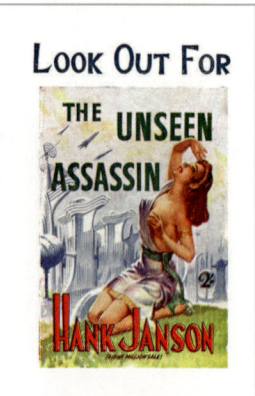
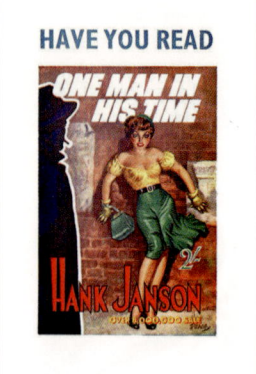

Reginald Heade's original cover painting for a *Hank Janson* novel entitled *Framed*. Clearly intended to be published by Top Fiction Press, which dates it to 1953, it did not appear at that time. Two years later, a novel of the same title was issued by Alexander Moring, but with a different Heade cover adapted from his earlier *Deadly Mission* piece as pictured opposite. The original *Framed* composition above was given a more chaste adaptation by a different, unknown artist for the cover of another 1955 Alexander Moring title, *Untamed*. It is unknown why, in his unused painting, Heade included a spine section much wider than the usual thickness of a pulp paperback, or why he incorporated the silhouette logo and publisher's name in a format unseen on any of the published novels. Possibly this was a try-out for a new cover format, ultimately unused, or even an idea for an abandoned hardback edition. (Image courtesy a private collector.)

A silhouette cover reissue of *This Woman is Death* (New Fiction Press, 1951)

SILHOUETTE COVER REISSUES

Early in 1951, New Fiction Press began issuing new editions of the Hank Janson novels, with graphic covers featuring just the silhouette logo and text. These reissues, the edition numbers of which seem to have been allocated on a fairly random basis, had the twin advantages of avoiding the cost of the full colour printing that would have been required in order to retain the original artwork (although there were such reprints done as well), and of reducing the risk of incurring further accusations of indecency. Presented over the following pages is a gallery of examples of these reissue covers, showing their minor variations in design and very wide range of colour schemes. Above: the '5th Edition' of *Lady, Mind That Corpse*.

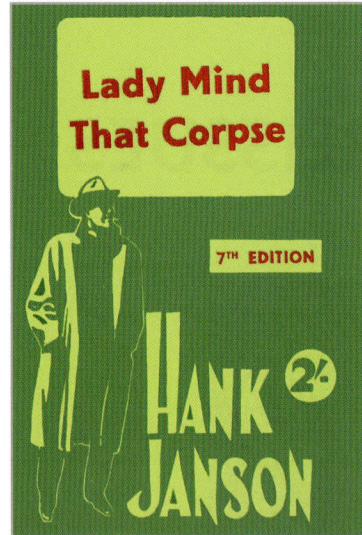

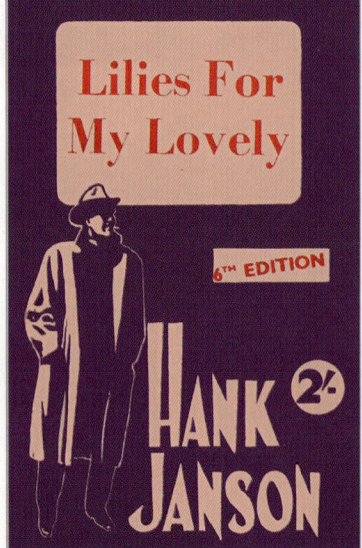
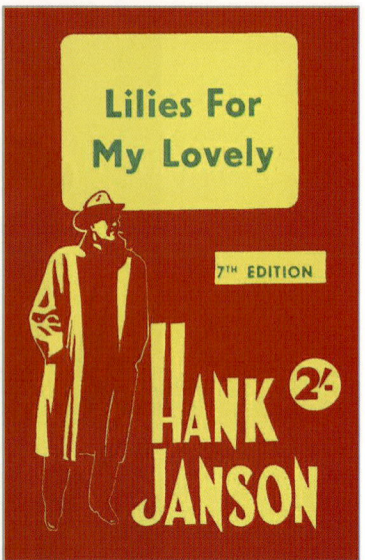
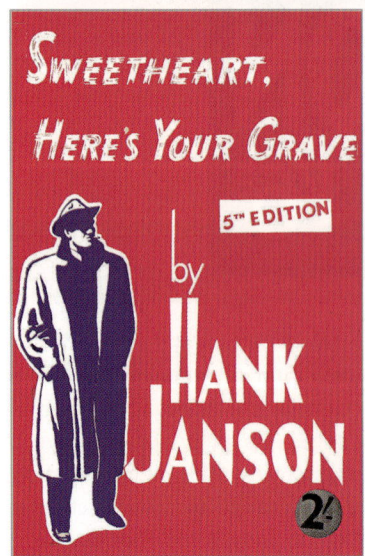
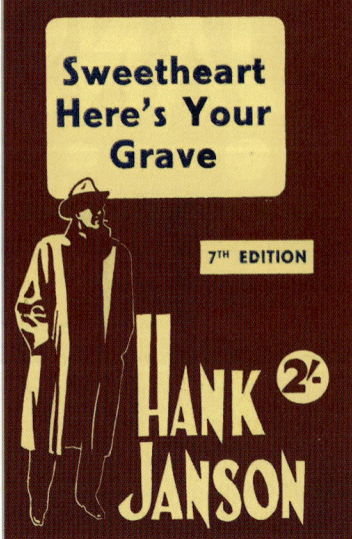
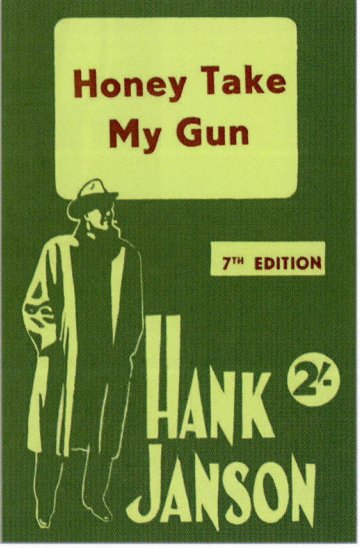

SILHOUETTE COVER REISSUES

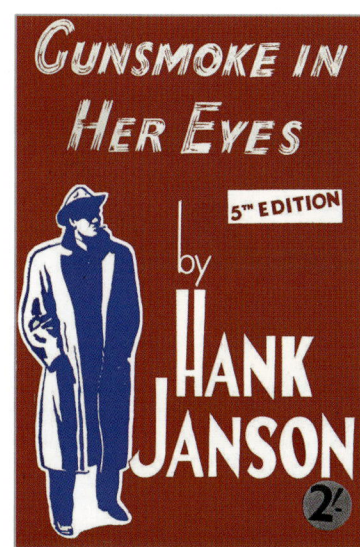
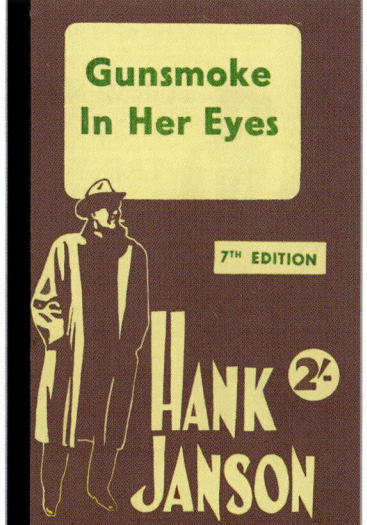

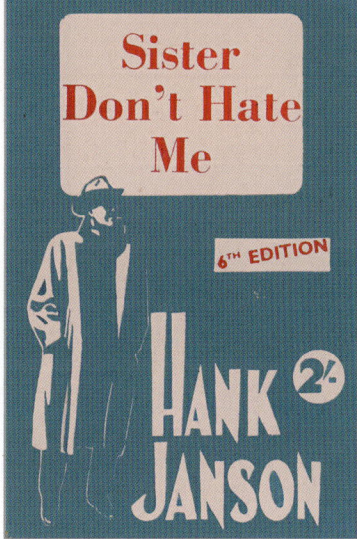
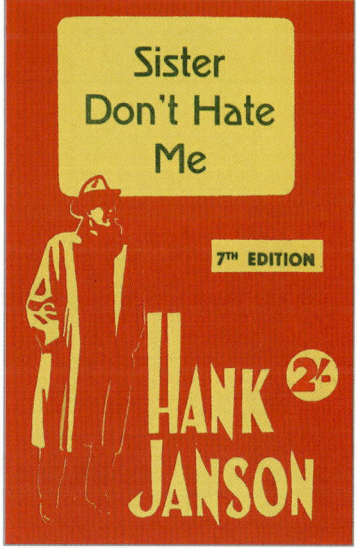

HANK JANSON UNDER COVER

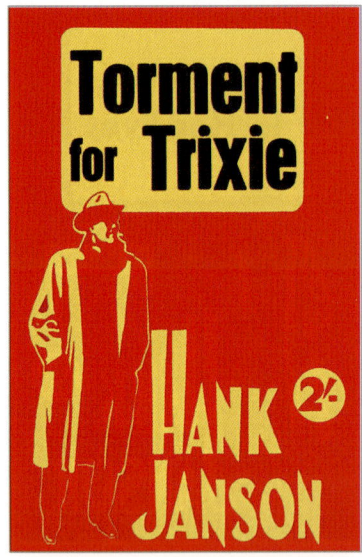  

The 1951-published reissue pictured above left is notable for using the spelling 'Trixie' on its front cover, whereas the text and title page – see above centre – still use 'Trixy', as in the book's first edition – see above right. For the 1952-published '7th Edition' version, the new spelling 'Trixie' was adopted throughout the book – see cover and title page shown to the right. It is unknown why this change was made. When the book was reissued by Roberts & Vinter in 1961, the title was altered again to *Suddenly It's Sin* (one of a number of instances of reissues being given new titles) – see page 133 – but this time the text reverted to 'Trixy' for the name of the character.

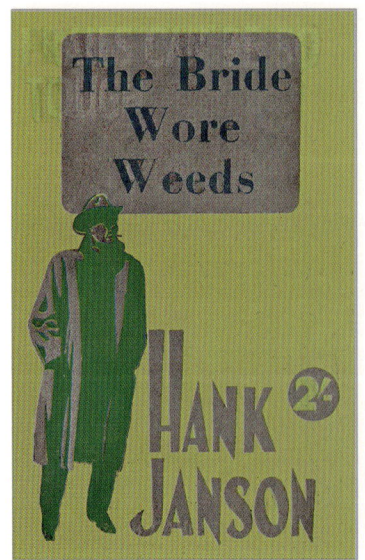 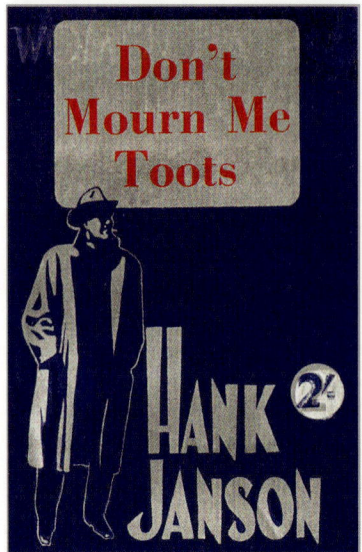

Sometimes, as a money- and paper-saving measure, unused excess copies of a silhouette-style cover originally intended for one book would be overprinted for use on another. Often in these cases, the original title lettering would remain faintly visible beneath the new. Two late-1951 examples of this are shown to the left. The covers for these reissues of *The Bride Wore Weeds* and *Don't Mourn Me Toots* can just be seen to have been overprinted – initially in silver only, then again to add colour – on spare copies of those for, respectively, *Frails Can Be So Tough* and *Women Hate Till Death* – two of the small number of first edition titles to have had silhouette covers.

SILHOUETTE COVER REISSUES

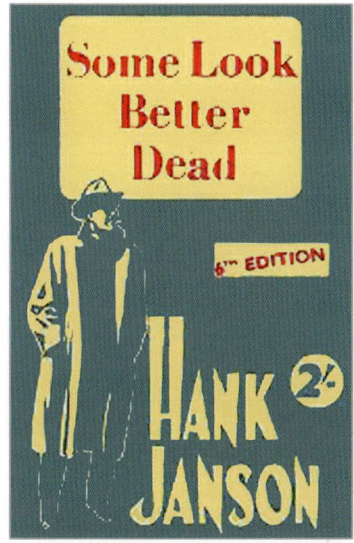

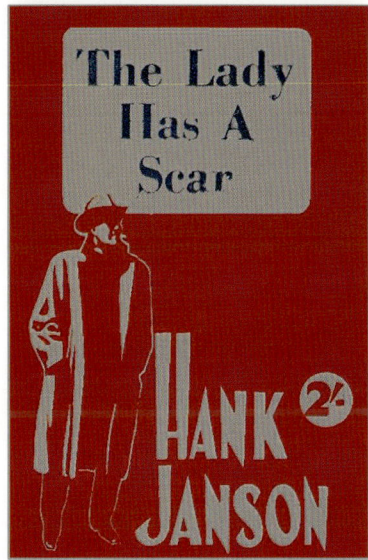

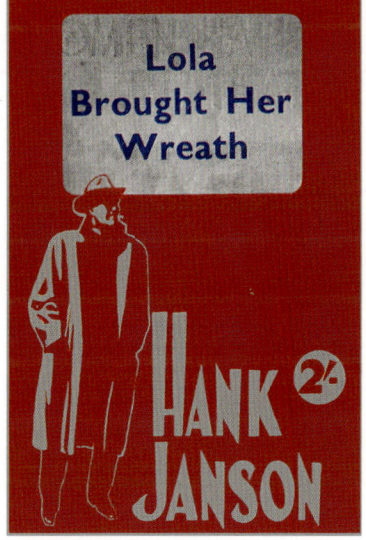
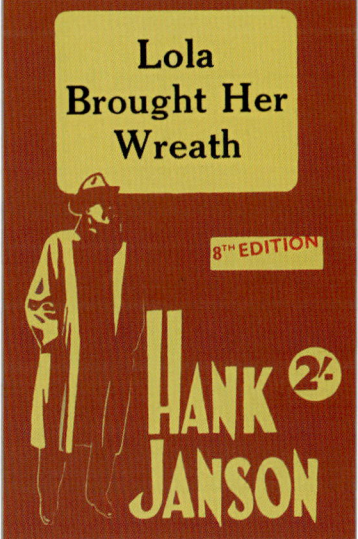

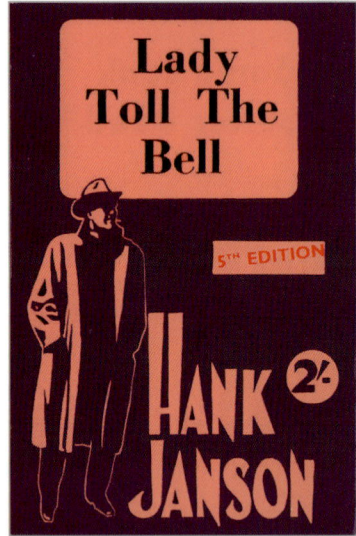
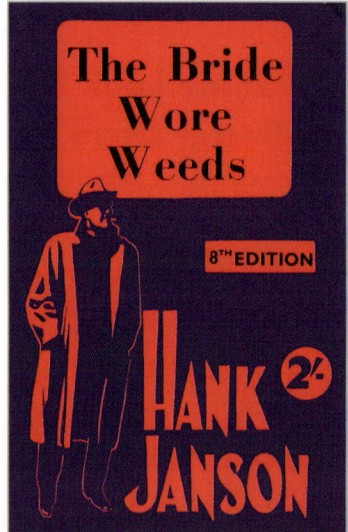
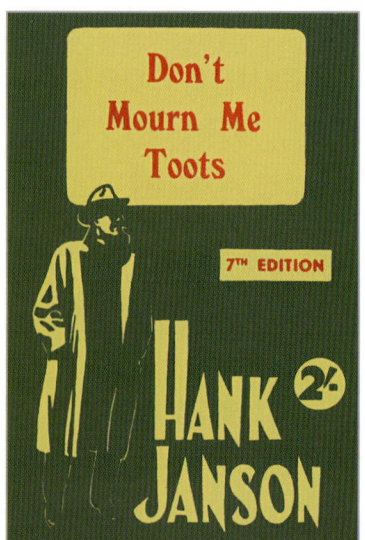
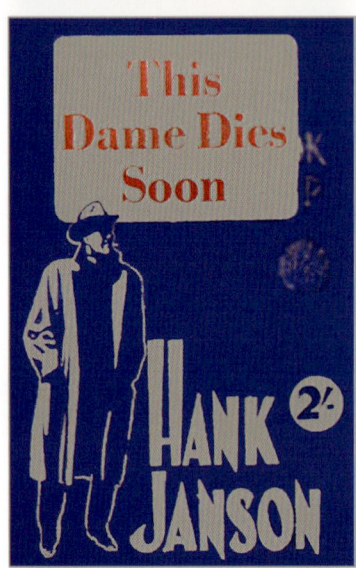
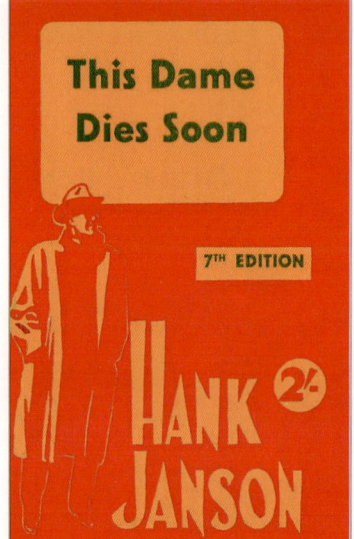

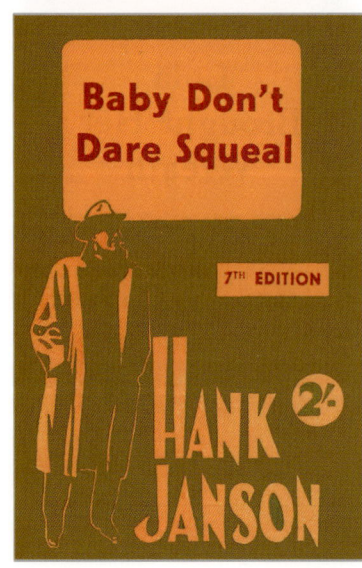

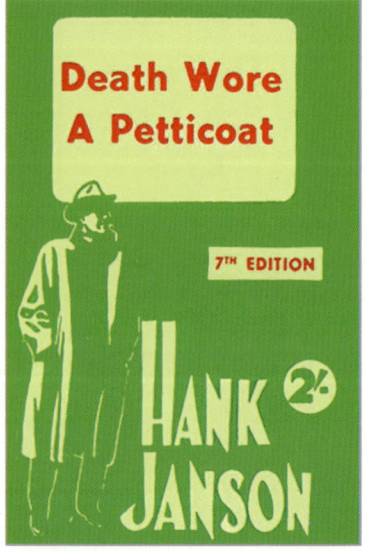

SILHOUETTE COVER REISSUES

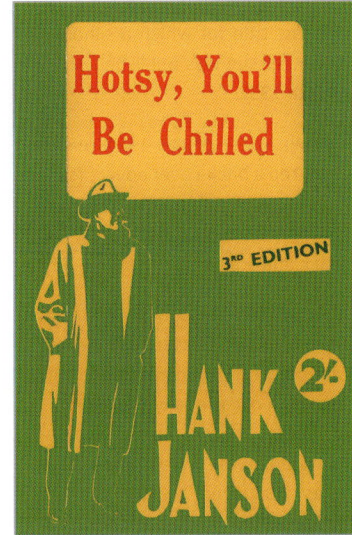
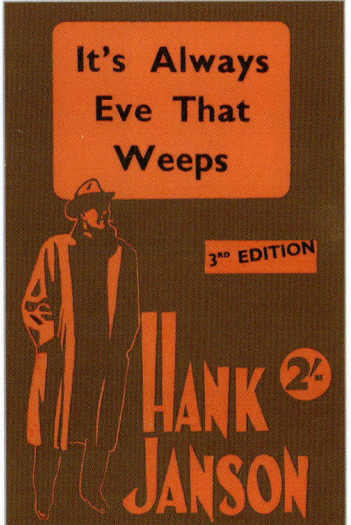
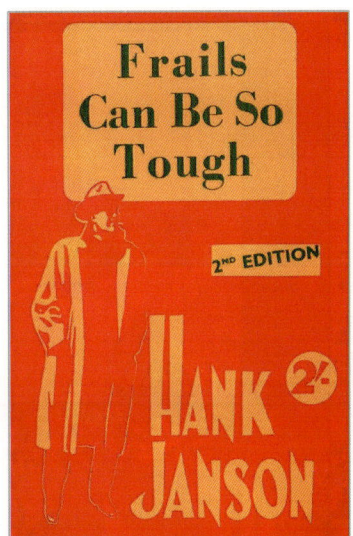

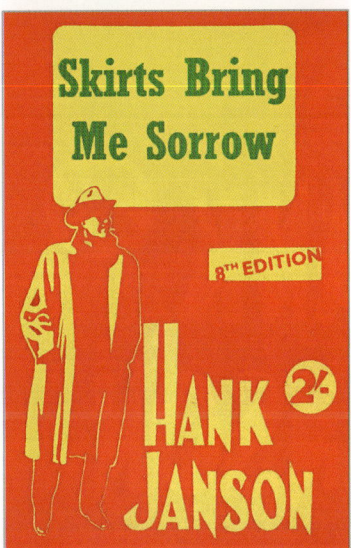

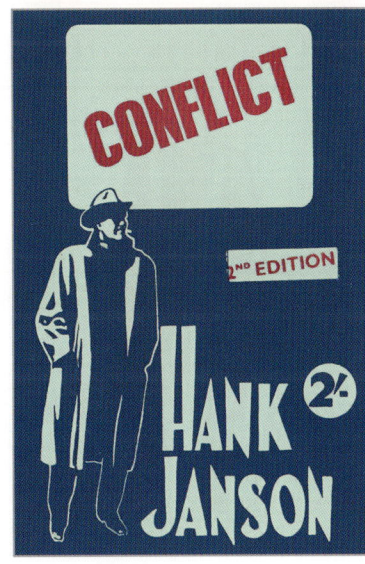
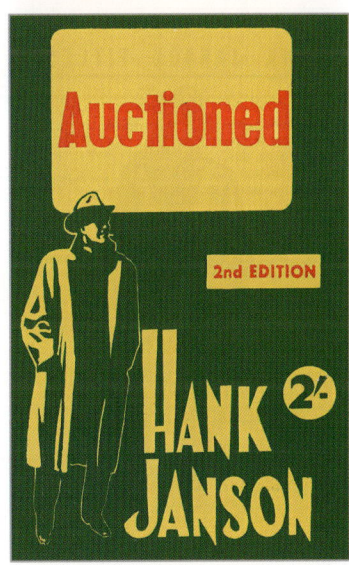

Left: *Tension* appears to have been the last title for which a silhouette cover reissue was published, in mid to late 1952.

Below: a few of the 1951 reissues featured a back-cover advert for the first issue of *Underworld* magazine, in various colours such as brown, black and – as pictured here – pink.

Bottom row: in most cases, the back covers of the reissues presented a standard Hank Janson titles listing, although occasionally these were in strikingly unusual colour schemes not seen on the novels' first editions – as illustrated by the examples shown here.

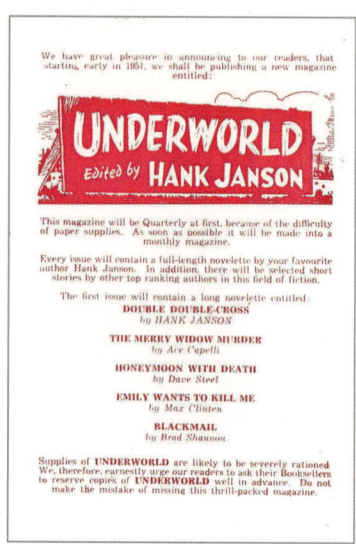

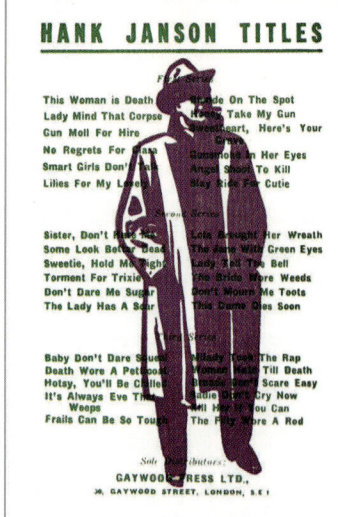

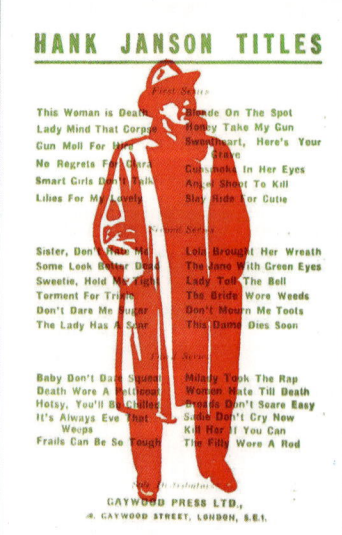

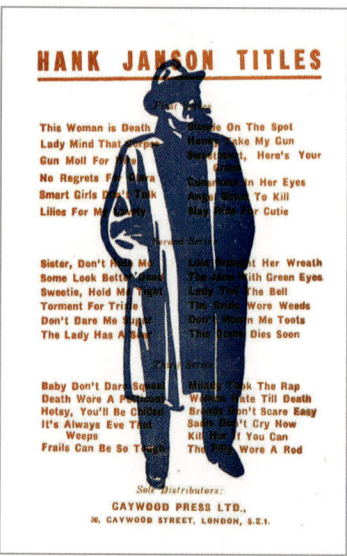

ALEXANDER MORING

Above: the version of the Hank Janson logo used throughout the Alexander Moring era.

Originally founded around the turn of the century, publishing company Alexander Moring was essentially defunct by the mid-1950s when, having completed an Obscene Publications Act prison sentence, Reginald Carter bought it to serve as a new outlet for Stephen Frances's Hank Janson novels. Between 1955 and 1959, fifty more titles were produced, some of them adapted reissues but the majority entirely new; the last four appeared under a different Carter-owned imprint, George Turton, but were to all intents and purposes part of the same run, although two of them – *Wild Girl* and *Torrid Temptress* – were by authors other than Frances, with whom Carter had by then fallen out over money. The books were if anything even more cheaply produced than the earlier New Fiction Press and Top Fiction Press ones, with the covers mostly printed on heavier card stock. Reginald Heade's services were also dispensed with at this time: three of the early Alexander Moring books do feature his work, but these were all instances of pre-existing paintings being reused; the remainder of the run had covers by other artists, identities unknown, either closely copying previous Heade pieces or else imitating his style. In every case but one – the true crime book *Jack Spot* – the artwork was placed below a distinctive red- and yellow-striped title panel.

Contraband (May 1955).

Untamed (1955).

Framed (September 1955). Reused art by Reginald Heade.

Tomorrow and a Day (November 1955).

Menace (1955). Art by Reginald Heade, adapted by another, unknown artist to make the female subject more fully clothed.

Deadly Mission (December 1955).

48 Hours (December 1955).

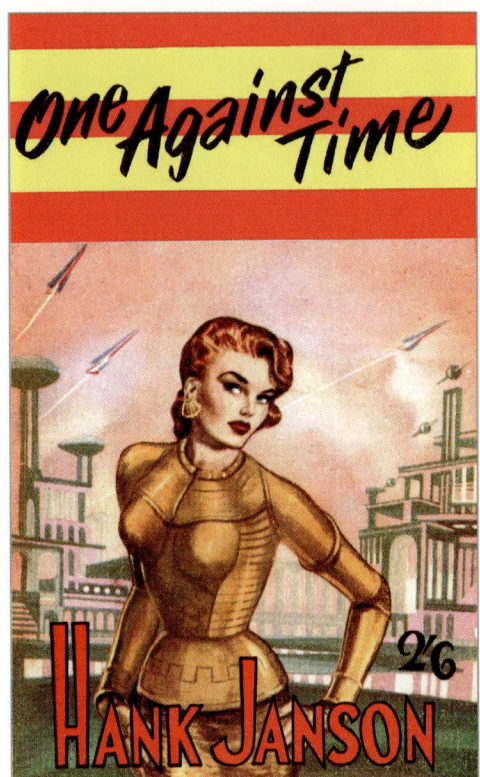
One Against Time (January 1956).

Devil's Highway (March 1956).

Hell's Angel (April 1955).

The Unseen Assassin (April 1956). Reused art by Reginald Heade (figure) and Ron Turner (background).

Escape (May 1956).

The Big Lie (1956).

Cactus (July 1956).

Bring Me Sorrow (1956).

They Die Alone (1956).

Strange Destiny (November 1956).

Tension (1957).

Bewitched (1957).

Whiplash (1957).

Conflict (1957).

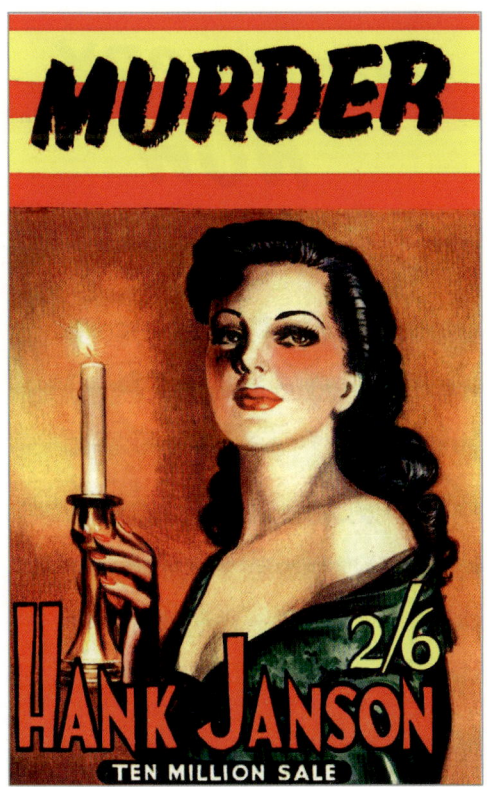

Murder (1957).

Sweet Fury (1957).

Hellcat (1957).

Persian Pride (September 1957).

Desert Fury (October 1957).

Don't Cry Now (1957).

ALEXANDER MORING

THE MOST SENSATIONAL,
DARING, EXCITING
AND DISTURBING
NOVEL
EVER WRITTEN
by HANK JANSON

ORDER NOW
"TOMORROW
AND A DAY"

A book which will shock you, frighten you, hold you breathless with an awful tension, yet will not permit you to lay it aside.

We warn you. Once you start to read this book you will not stop until the last page is turned and the book placed reluctantly on the shelf to be read again later.

READY SOON

2s 6d.

Top left: the Moring-era titles resumed the practice of presenting back-cover titles listings – now with a more striking background in the distinctive red- and yellow-striped colour scheme.

Above and centre left: the books' back pages often advertised Moring's forthcoming Hank Janson titles, as in these examples.

Below: a contemporary promotional blotter, including a calendar for the last six months of 1957. (Image courtesy Steve Chibnall.)

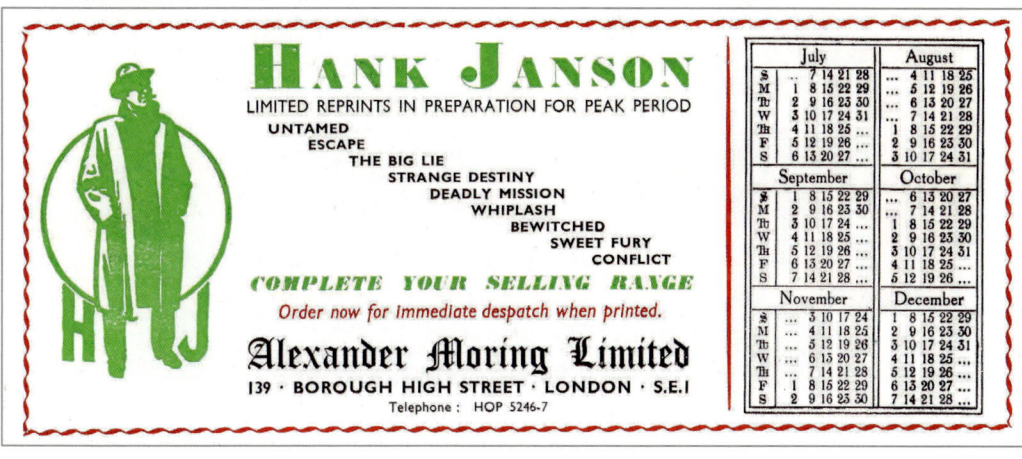

Enemy of Men (1957), featuring the Hank Janson silhouette figure as a looming background shadow.

Sinister Rapture (October 1957).

Revolt (November 1957).

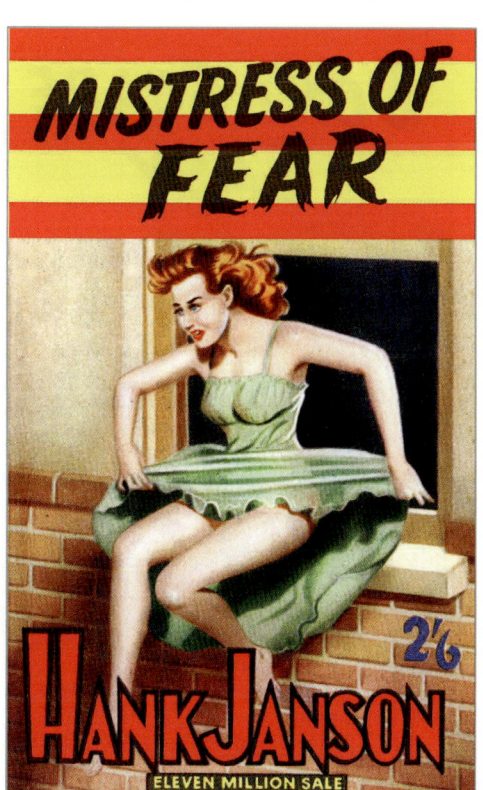

Mistress of Fear (February 1958).

Too Soon to Die (1958).

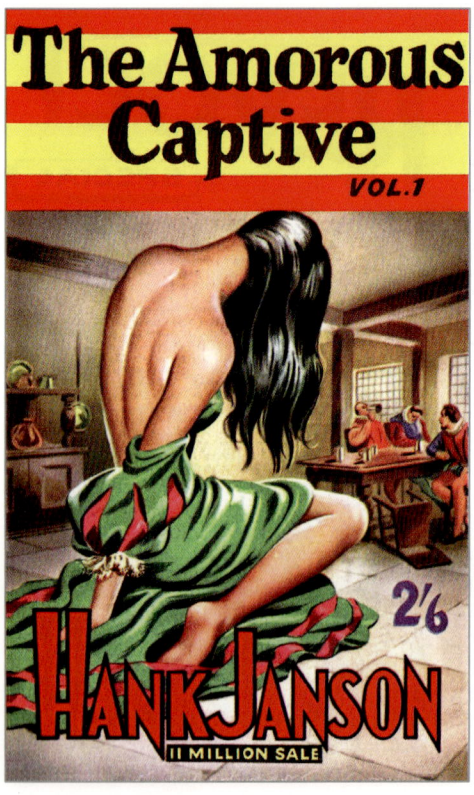

The Amorous Captive Vol. 1 (1958).

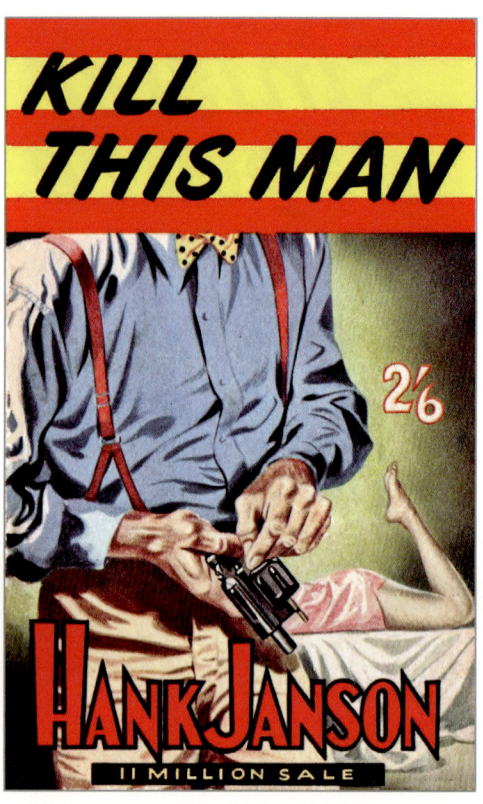

Kill This Man (May 1958).

Lose This Gun (1958).

Don't Scare Easy (1958).

Flight from Fear (1958).

An unusual Alexander Moring-era item was a large-format Hank Janson 'crime comic album' – essentially a graphic novel – called *Hank - the Statuette and the Englishman*, in which a young woman visits Hank at his *Chicago Chronicle* office and seeks his help to find her missing brother – during which exploit she often ends up semi-undressed. Shown above are the cover and three example pages, including the first and the last. The crude, poorly-printed artwork was uncredited, but notable for including a depiction of Hank himself. It is uncertain exactly when in the 1950s this album was issued – the publisher's address on the last page is different from that given in the Moring novels, although very nearby. It could even have preceded the novels.

Situation – Grave! (September 1958).

Sugar and Vice (May 1958).

Hate (1958).

Avenging Nymph (January 1959).

Jack Spot (December 1958), the only Alexander Moring-era book to depart from the standard cover format.

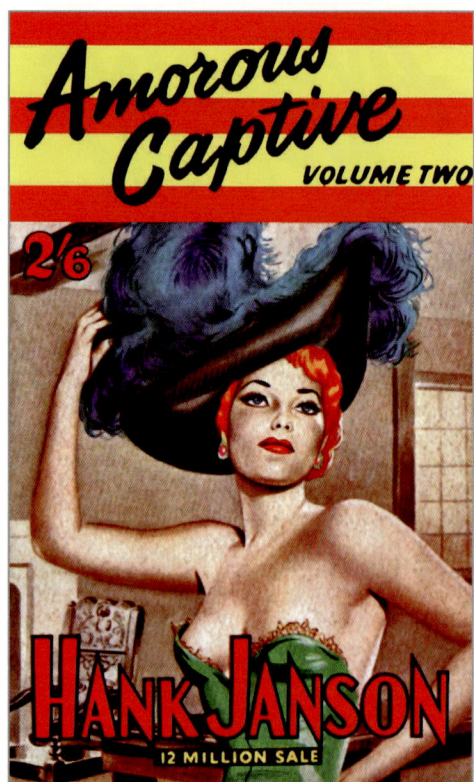

Amorous Captive Volume Two (February 1959).

Invasion (1959).

ALEXANDER MORING

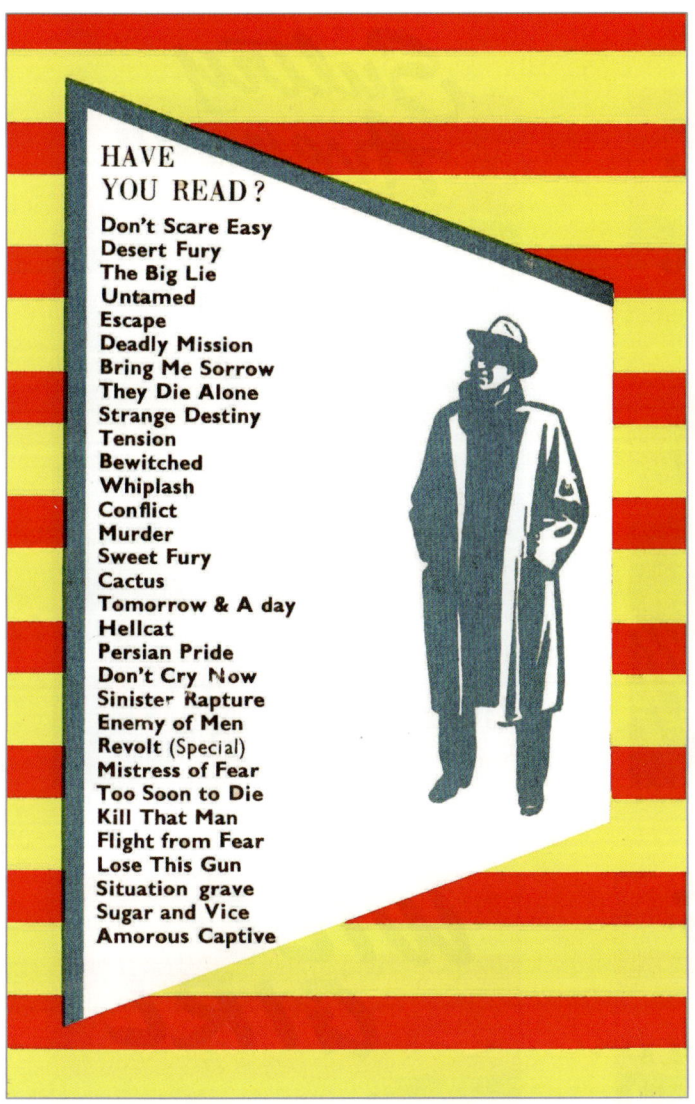

Top left: by 1958, the standard back-cover listing of the Alexander Moring range had grown to the point where not all the titles could be included.

Above: the books' title pages revealed the switch of imprints from Alexander Moring to George Turton for the last four novels in this run; but in other respects the format remained unchanged.

Left: further examples of the type of adverts that appeared in the Alexander Moring books' back pages to promote forthcoming titles.

Silken Snare (May 1959).

Sultry Avenger (June 1959).

Amorous Captive Vol 3 (August 1959).

Wild Girl (September 1959).

Torrid Temptress (1959)

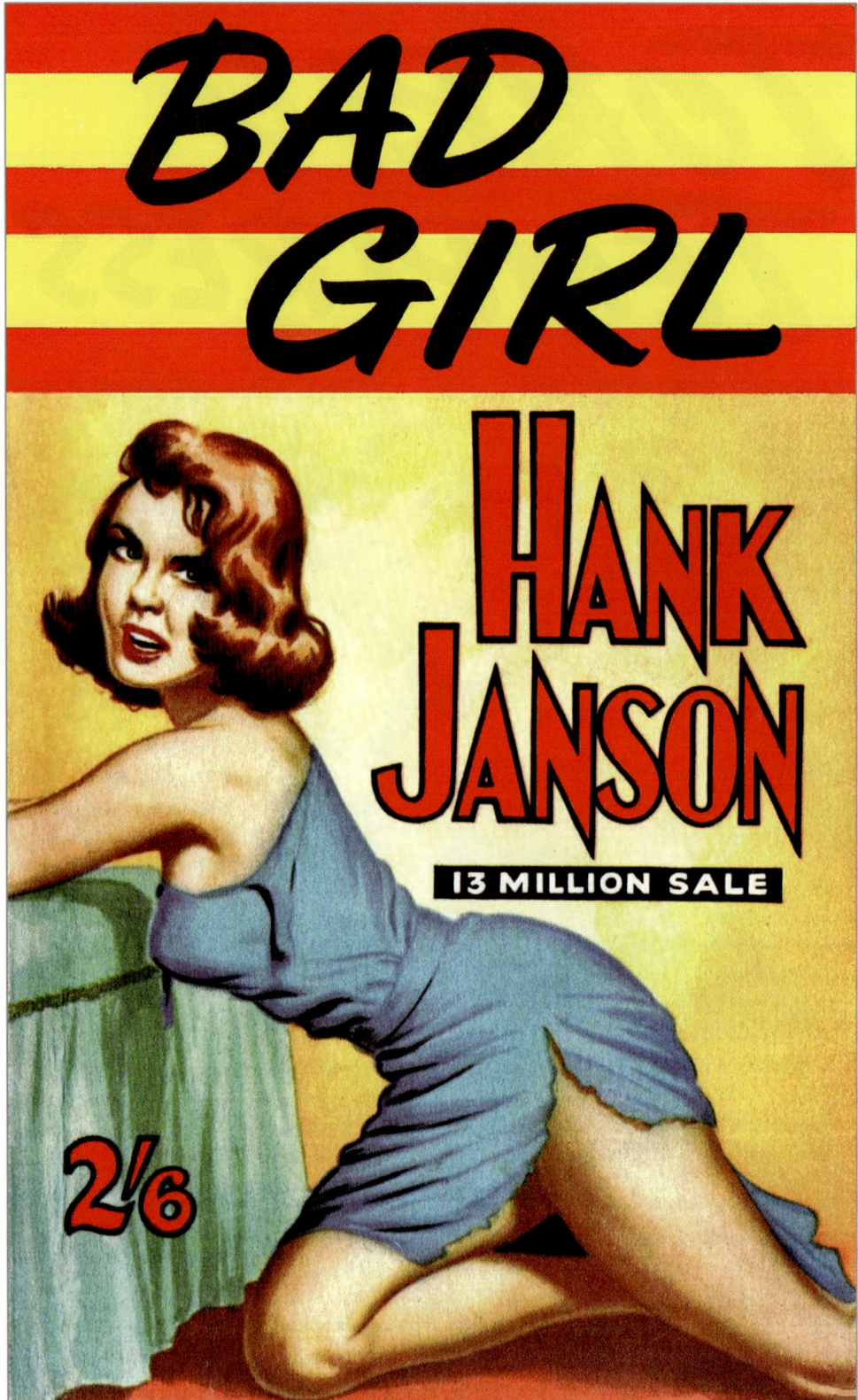

Bad Girl (November 1959), the final Alexander Moring-era novel – actually published, like the preceding three, under the alternative Reginald Carter imprint George Turton.

ROBERTS & VINTER

Above: the small logo that Roberts & Vinter began placing in the top right-hand corner of their Hank Janson covers from late 1960 onwards.

In October 1959, having fallen out with the character's creator and hitherto principal author Stephen Frances, Reginald Carter sold the rights to Hank Janson to a new company formed by wholesaler and one-time chef Jim Roberts and his business manager Derek Vinter. Curiously, the pair's first two Janson releases, *All Tramps are Trouble* and *Obsession*, claimed on their title pages to have been published by the – apparently fictitious – Universal Publishing Corporation, Tangier. Subsequent novels, however, appeared under the new Roberts & Vinter imprint. Authors for this latest run included Harry Hobson, Harold Kelly and Victor Norwood, although Stephen Frances's work continued to feature, initially in the form of retitled reissues but eventually via further original novels, as Frances reluctantly came round to the idea of working with the new rights-holders. Roberts & Vinter must have bought not only the rights to Hank Janson but also the unsold stock of earlier Alexander Moring and George Turton titles, as they proceeded to market the latter as well, in some cases with the original covers stripped off and new ones substituted.

Many of the cover paintings for this new range were provided by the excellent London-based artist Michel Atkinson, who had a French mother and an English father; his contributions are certainly the best of those produced after Reginald Heade's time. Most of the others are believed to have been supplied by various Italian and Spanish freelancers. The artists' identities, where confirmed, are noted in this section's illustration captions.

All Tramps Are Trouble (1959). Art by Chirry.

Obsession (1959).

Cupid Turns Killer! (1960). Art by Chirry.

Slaves for Seduction (1960). Art by Chirry.

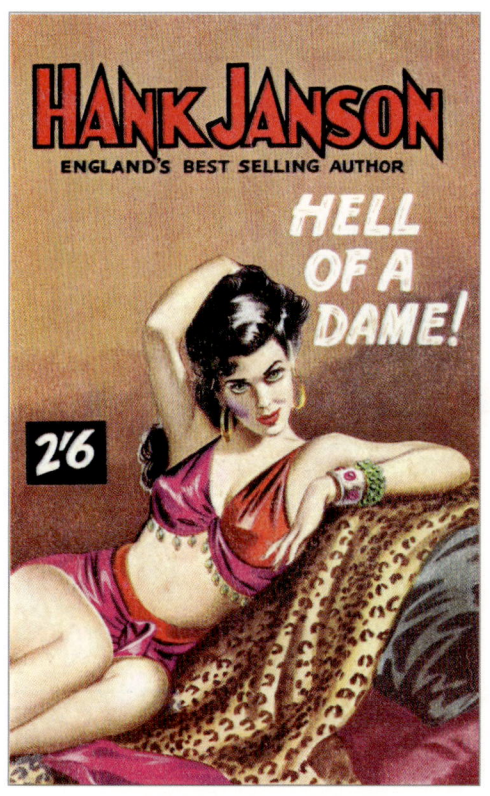
Hell of a Dame! (1960).

This Wicked Sex (1960).

Quiet Waits the Grave (1960). Art by Fernando Carcupino.

Ripe for Rapture! (1960). Art by Fernando Carcupino.

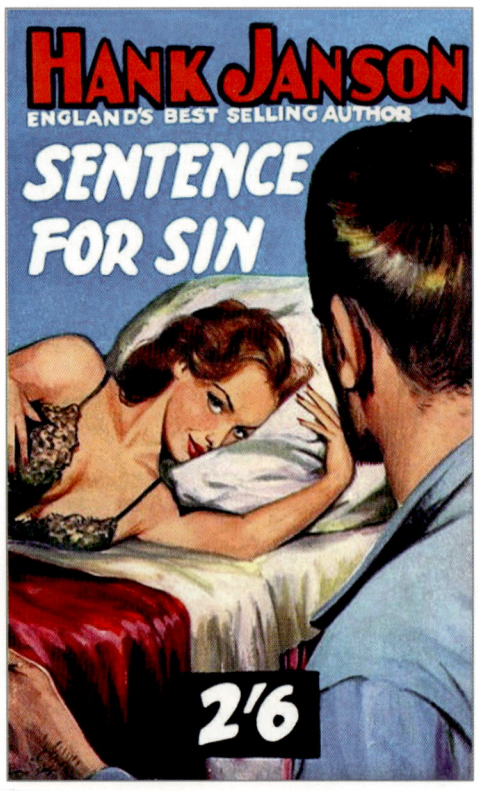

Sentence for Sin (1960).

This Hood for Hire (1960).

Beloved Traitor (1960).

'Come Quickly, Honey' (1960).

Ecstasy (1960). Art by Fernando Carcupino.

Cutie on Call (1960).

Passionate Waif (1960).

Secret Session (1960).

Fireball (1960).

Cool Sugar (1960).

HANK JANSON UNDER COVER

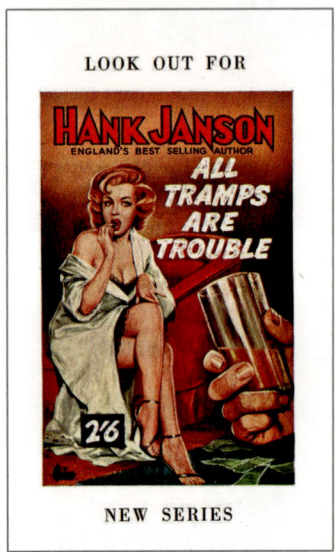

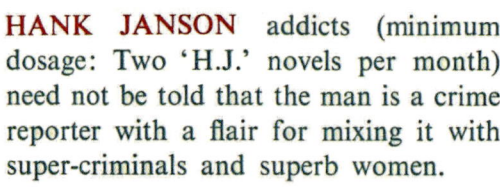 HANK JANSON addicts (minimum dosage: Two 'H.J.' novels per month) need not be told that the man is a crime reporter with a flair for mixing it with super-criminals and superb women.

Born in London, Hank moved off around the world in search of action and adventure, and found his real talent as a writer after being washed up in Chicago. When he eventually quit full-time reportage to become one of the most prolific story-writers in the English language, he had lived through enough excitement to fill a thousand books.

 His present whereabouts are never disclosed.

SECURITY, you know.

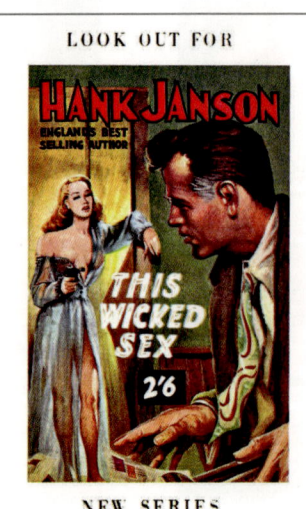

The first few Roberts & Vinter books, in identical fashion to the last few classic-era ones, had back cover adverts that promoted forthcoming titles by way of images of their front cover artwork – typical examples are shown to the left. Then, though, came a short run of books that all featured the back cover text shown above, giving brief background information about Hank Janson alongside the familiar silhouette logo – still being used a decade after it was originally designed by Philip Mendoza.

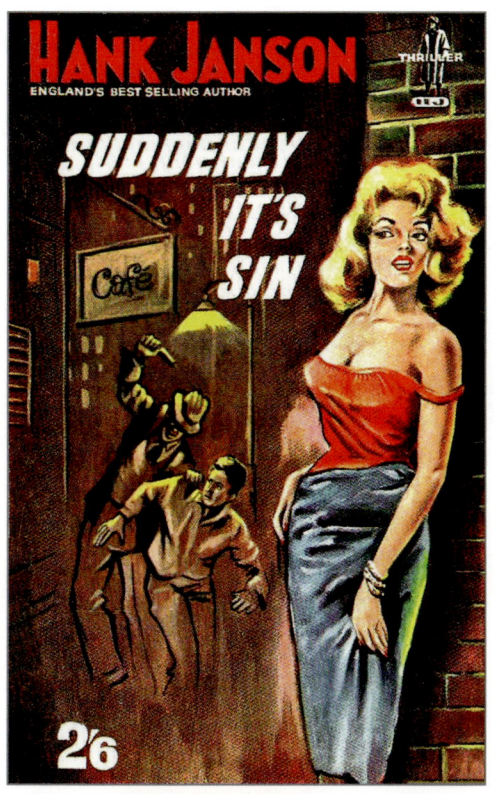
Suddenly It's Sin (1961).

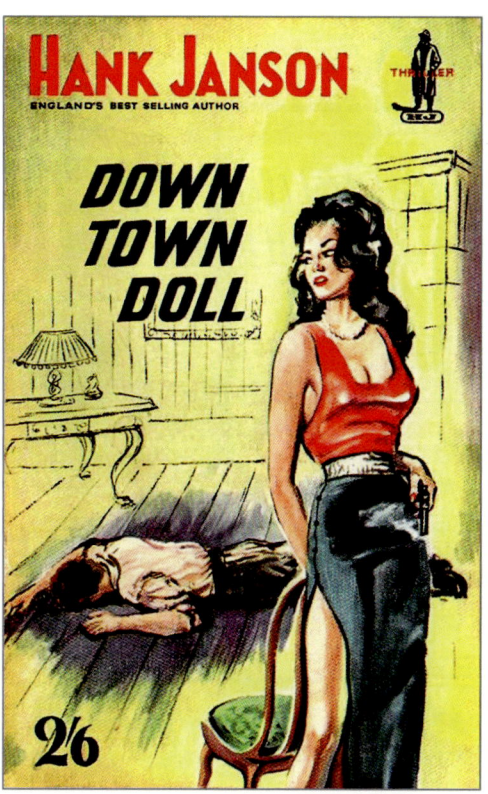
Downtown Doll (1961).

Late Night Revel (March 1961). (Image courtesy Steve Chibnall.)

Outcast (1961).

Delicious Danger (1961).

Prey for a Newshawk (1961).

Destination – Dames (May 1961).

Janson Go Home! (1961).

FOLLOW THIS MAN!

You don't need a bloodhound to tell you that when you're on to a good thing you stick to it.

That's why there are so many people around who make a point of buying a new HANK JANSON whenever they see one.

What's the infallible recipe?

Experience, mainly. Before becoming a full-time writer, H.J. packed a lifetime of adventure, romance and thrills into the few years it took him to hit the top in the States as a Chicago Crime Correspondent.

A man with talent and a store-house of experience like that never lacks the right kind of authentic inspiration. You follow?

Over to you, HANK!

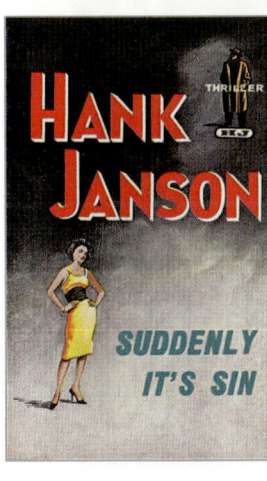

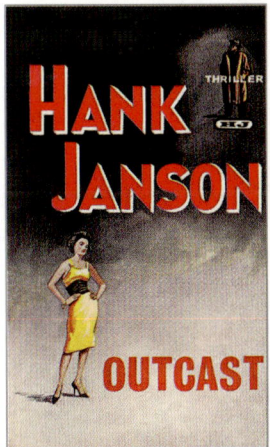
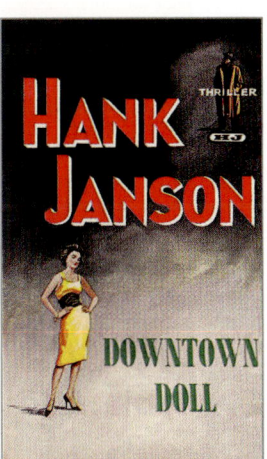

Top right: in mid-1961, this new standard back cover blurb began to be used in place of the one that first appeared a few months earlier.

Other images on this page: several of the books first published in 1960 and 1961 were subsequently reissued by Roberts & Vinter with this generic new cover design. This may have been seen as the start of a more extensive reissue range, akin to the silhouette cover reissues of the early 1950s. If so, however, it would seem the idea was soon abandoned, leaving only a few examples.

Scent from Heaven (1961). Art by Michel Atkinson.

Crowns Can Kill (1961).

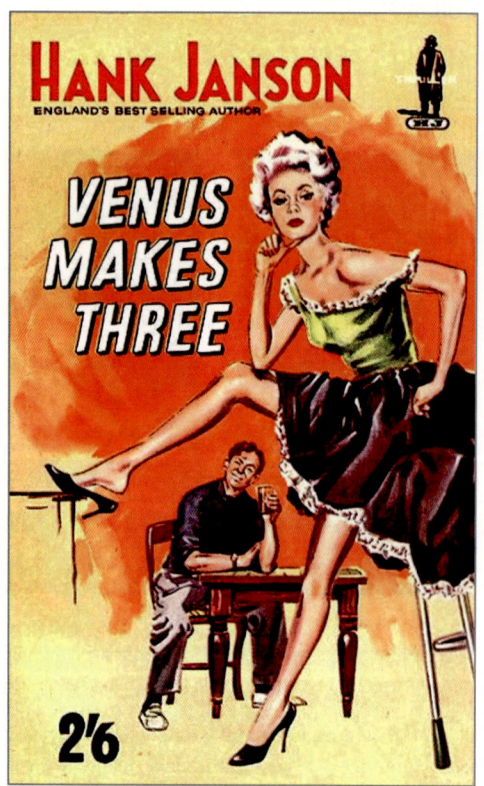
Venus Makes Three (1961).

Don't Scare Easy (1961). Art by Michel Atkinson.

She Sleeps to Conquer (1961). Art by Michel Atkinson.

Lose This Gun (1961). Art by Michel Atkinson.

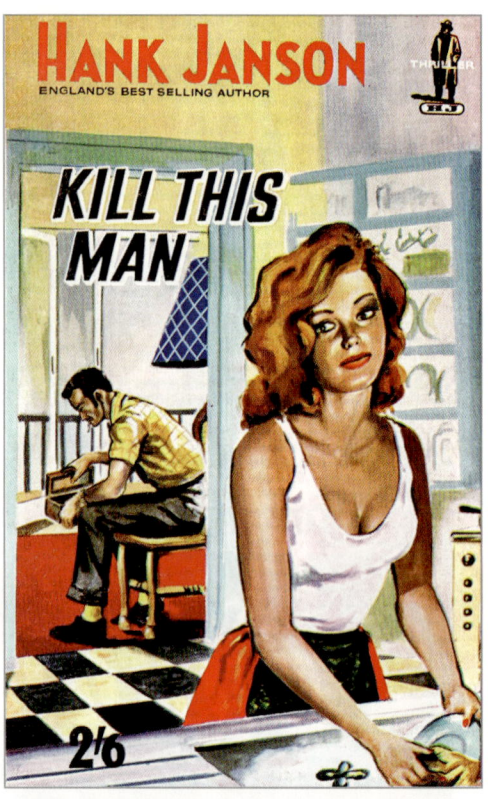
Kill This Man (1961). Art by Michel Atkinson.

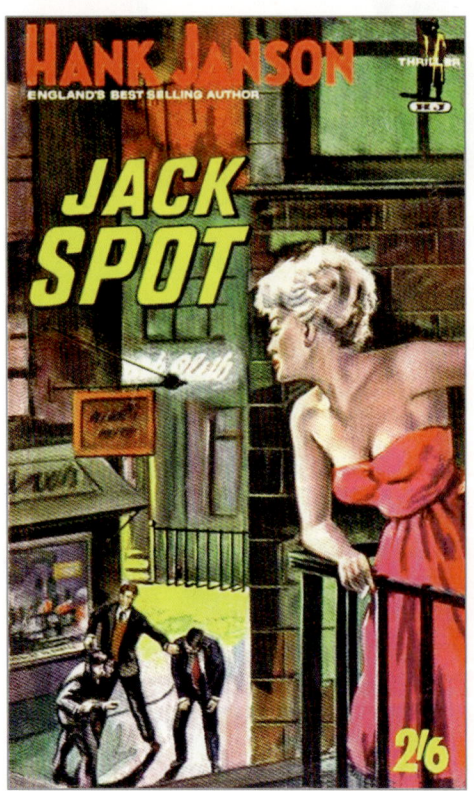
Jack Spot (October 1961).

Reluctant Hostess (October 1961).

Short-Term Wife (October 1961).

Lady, Lie Low (1961). Art by Michel Atkinson.

Mastermind (1961). Art by Michel Atkinson.

Hell's Belles (1961). Art by Michel Atkinson.

Break for a Lovely (1961).

ROBERTS & VINTER

COOL SUGAR

by

HANK JANSON

Published by
ROBERTS and VINTNER Ltd.,
44, Milkwood Road, London, S.E.24.

THIS MONTH
and
EVERY MONTH
NEW
TITLES
by
Hank Janson

Look out for

RAVE FOR A ROUGHNECK
SHE WOLF
CRIME ON MY HANDS

2/6 EACH

You can Place a Regular Order with Your Usual Newsagent for New Hank Janson Titles

Just cut out this form and hand it to your supplier with your requirements marked.

STANDING ORDER FOR HANK JANSON BOOKS

Please supply until further notice, one copy of each new Hank Janson novel as published.

Name ....
Address ....
....
....

Complete this part if you wish to order earlier titles as advertised

Please supply one copy of the following titles:

....
....
....
....

HANK JANSON NEW "60" SERIES

Have you read all the new-style Hank Janson with the full picture covers?

Obsession	Suddenly its Sin
All Tramps Are Trouble	Downtown Doll
Cupid Turns Killer	Late Night Revel
Slaves For Seduction	Outcast
The Wicked Sex	Delicious Danger
Hell of a Dame	Prey for a Newshawk
Ripe for Rapture	Janson Go Home
This Hood for Hire	Destination Dames
Sentence for Sin	Scent from Heaven
Come Quickly Honey	She Sleeps to Conquer
Beloved Traitor	Crowns Can Kill
Passionate Waif	Master Mind
Ecstasy	Lady Lie Low
Secret Session	Hell's Belles
Cutie on Call	Break for a Lovely
Cool Sugar	Play it Quiet
Fireball	Beauty and the Beat

Obtain these now from Your Local Bookshop or Newsagent

2/6 EACH

Read a "HANK JANSON" every week!

Your Local Newsagent or Bookseller can supply the following titles now.

Conflict	Lose this Gun
Menace	They Die Alone
Hellcat	Persian Pride
Murder	Devil's Highway
Tension	Too Soon to Die
Revolt	Will this Man
Invasion	Sugar and Vice
Hate	Sultry Avenger
Bad Girl	Bring Me Sorrow
Desert Fury	Don't Scare Easy
Sweet Fury	Mistress of Fear
Jack Spot	Avenging Nymph
Wild Girl	Flight from Fear
Hell's Angel	Torrid Temptress
Big Lie	Situation Grave

2/6 EACH

Top left: the Roberts & Vinter title pages had exactly the same layout as the Alexander Moring ones. Other images: as time went by, the closing pages of the Roberts & Vinter books began featuring increasing numbers of adverts like these, tempting readers to buy or place a regular order for other titles in the range. Sometimes, up to three such adverts would be included at the back of a single book. The one at bottom right notably lists some earlier Alexander Moring titles that Roberts & Vinter were still marketing.

Play It Quiet (1962).

Beauty and the Beat (1962).

Rave for a Roughneck (1962).

She Wolf (1962).

Chicago Chick (1962). Art by Michel Atkinson.

Uncover Agent (1962). Art by Michel Atkinson.

Crime on My Hands (1962). Art by Michel Atkinson.

Flight from Fear (1962). Art by Michel Atkinson.

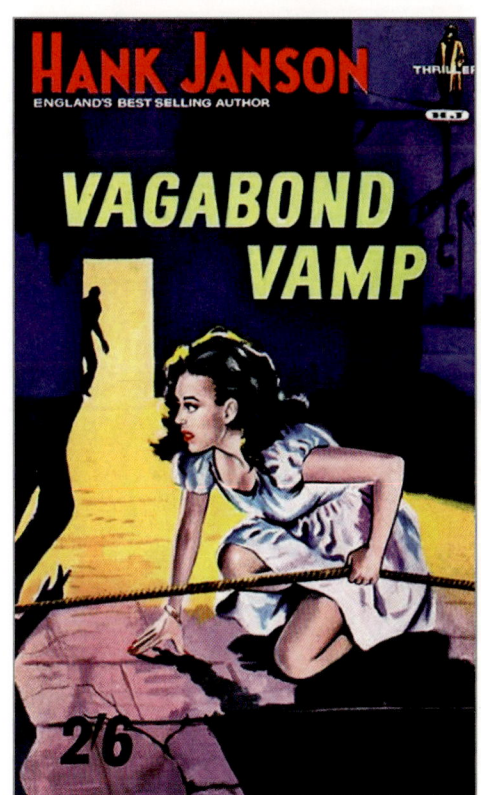
Vagabond Vamp (1962).

Take This – Sweetie (1962).

Honey for Me (1962). Art by Michel Atkinson.

Mistress of Fear (1962). Art by Michel Atkinson.

Too Soon to Die (1962). Art by Michel Atkinson.

Run for Lover (1962).

Like Crazy (1962). Art by Michel Atkinson.

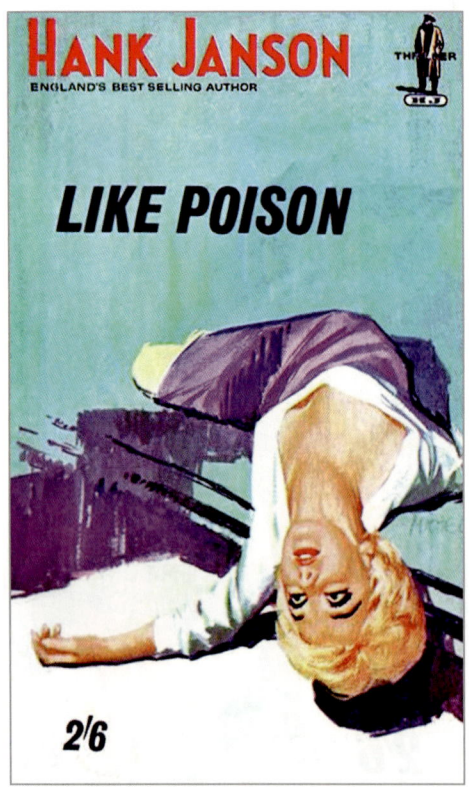
Like Poison (1962). Art by Michel Atkinson.

Kill Me for Kicks (1962).

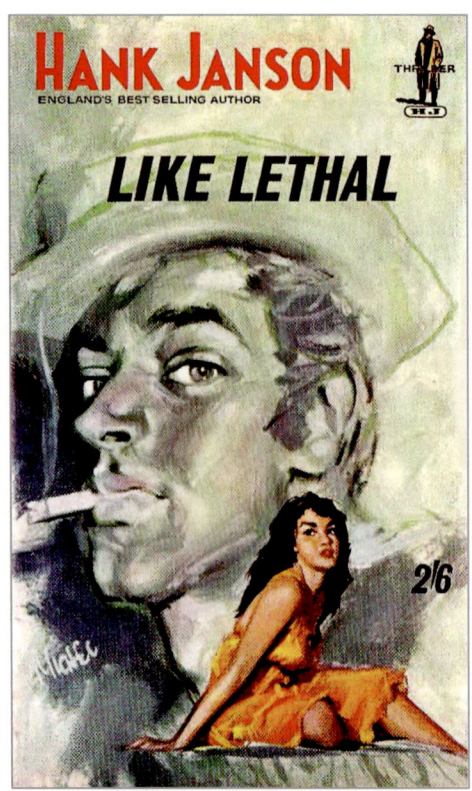
Like Lethal (1962). Art by Michel Atkinson.

Twist for Two (1962).

Blood Bath (1962). Art by Michel Atkinson.

Dig Those Heels (1962).

Grape Vine (1962).

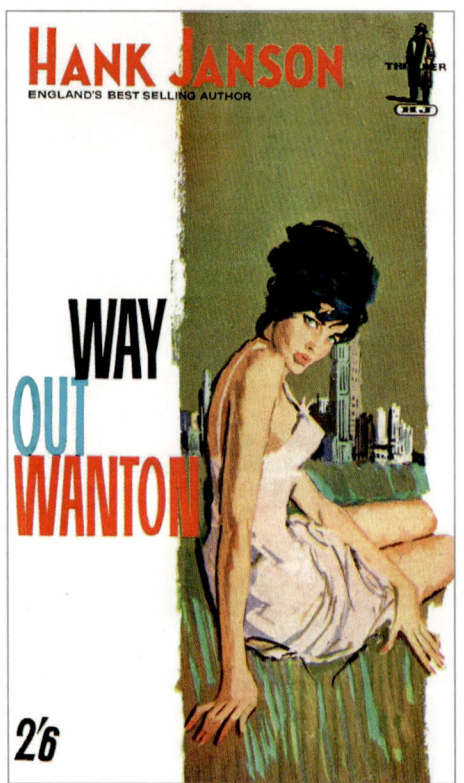
Way Out Wanton (1962).

Savage Sequel (1962). Art by Rafael Cortiella.

Nymph in the Night (1962). Art by Michel Atkinson.

Uncommon Market (1962). Art by Michel Atkinson.

Dateline – Diane (1962). Art by Michel Atkinson.

In 1962, Roberts & Vinter resumed their practice of marketing old Alexander Moring-era stock with the original covers stripped off and new ones substituted. Unlike before, these re-covered books were not presented as part of the main range, but were issued alongside it. They were some of the last Hank Janson titles to be sold at 2/6, before the price was increased to 3/6. Money was saved, however, by not affording them all new pieces of cover art; instead, four generic paintings were commissioned and each used for several different titles, as shown above and opposite. One of the four (top left) was by Rafael Cortiella (1931-), a Barcelona-born artist who had worked extensively throughout Europe, and the others by Joan Beltrán Bofill aka Noiquet (1934-2009), another Spanish artist, who outside of his commercial work painted mainly in the impressionist style.

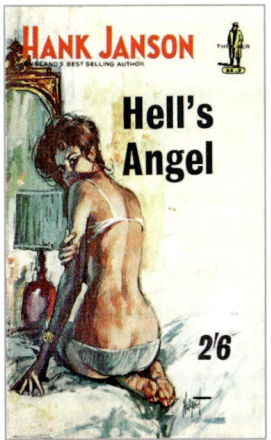
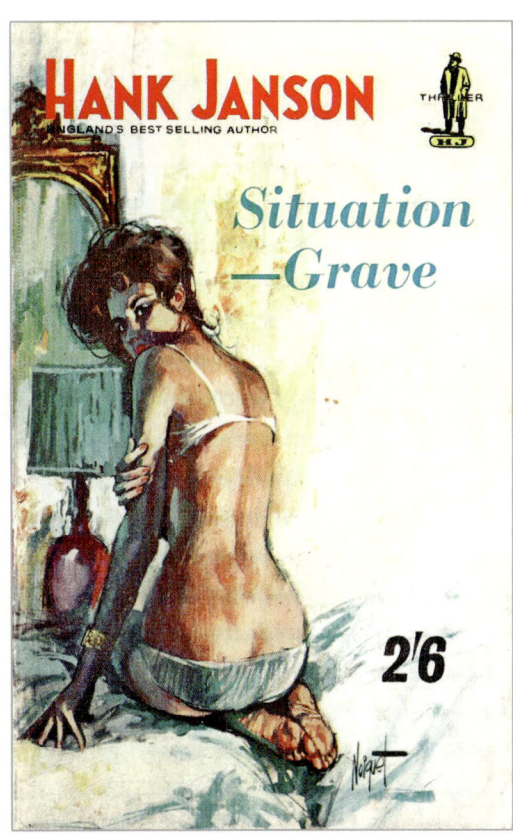

Below: toward the end of 1962, from *Way Out Wanton* onwards, the spines of the Roberts & Vinter books – including, as shown in these examples, all of that year's re-covered Alexander Moring-era reissues – were given a striking new design; before, they had consisted simply of standard black text against a plain white background.

Exclusive! (1962).

Angel Astray (1962).

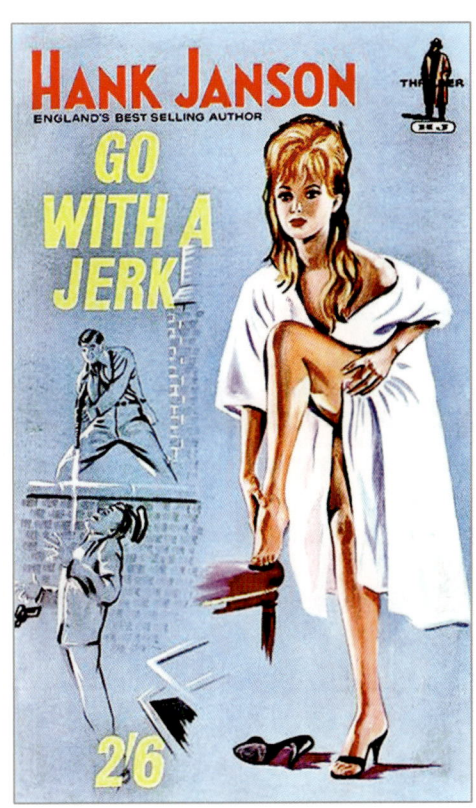
Go With a Jerk (1962).

Passion Pact (1963).

Dateline Darlene (1963). Art by Michel Atkinson.

Above: *Second String* (1963), the last Roberts & Vinter novel to be issued before the advent of the company's new Compact imprint. Art by Joan Beltrán Bofill, working under the name Noiquet.

Above right: another new regular back-cover blurb was introduced in 1962, appearing from *Uncommon Market* on.

Right: Hank Janson's creator Stephen Frances returned to the range in 1962 with *Nymph in the Night*, following this up in 1963 with *Second String*.

Bottom right: *Second String* was notable for the introduction of a new character, Hilary Brand, who – as clearly signalled by this advert printed at the back of the book – was intended from the start to return in the Compact titles.

COMPACT

Above: the evolving spine design of the Compact-era novels is illustrated by this selection of titles dating from 1963 to 1970.

In 1963, Jim Roberts decided to give up publishing in favour of pursuing new challenges. Consequently Roberts & Vinter was sold to entrepreneur Godfrey Gold – who had played a peripheral part in the Hank Janson story for some years, as a wholesaler working with Julius Reiter and Reginald Carter – and his business partner and fellow wholesaler David Warburton. The pair soon decided to relaunch the range in a 'New Style "64" Series' (as opposed to the 'New "60" Series' begun when Roberts & Vinter first acquired the rights), now under the Compact imprint, publishing at a rate of more than one book per month. As most of Gold's time was taken up with his East End family's many other business ventures (some of them run by his son David, now best known as co-chairman of West Ham football club), day-to-day management of the range in practice fell mainly to Warburton, aided initially by Derek Vinter, who stayed with the company for a time after Roberts' departure, then by up-and-coming writer and editor Michael Moorcock. Harry Hobson, Harold Kelly, Victor Norwood and Stephen Frances were now joined by Jim Moffatt and latterly Colin Fraser as authors of the novels. Just as the last four Alexander Moring titles had appeared under the alternative George Turton imprint, so the last dozen of this run came out as Gold & Warburton books rather than as Roberts & Vinter ones, although still under the company's Compact imprint. The only other difference was the stories' increasingly explicit content. By this time, artwork covers had already been dropped in favour of unappealing photographic ones. Then, in 1971, with sales rapidly dwindling, the range finally petered out and came to a rather ignominious end.

I for Intrigue (1963). Art by Michel Atkinson.

Sensuality (1963). Art by Michel Atkinson.

Dateline Debbie (1963). Art by Michel Atkinson.

Brand Image (1963). Art by Michel Atkinson.

COMPACT

Heartache (1963). Art by Michel Atkinson.

The Love Makers (1963). Art by Rafael Cortiella.

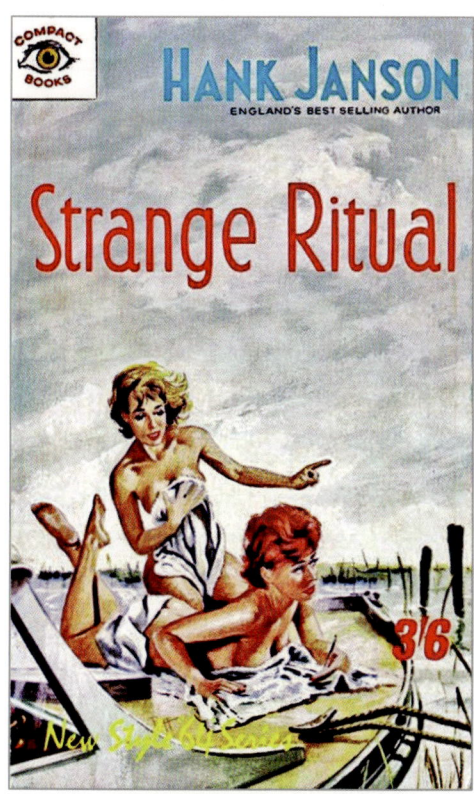

Strange Ritual (1963). Art by Sam Peffer.

Hilary's Terms (1963). Art by Michel Atkinson.

Nerve Centre (1963).

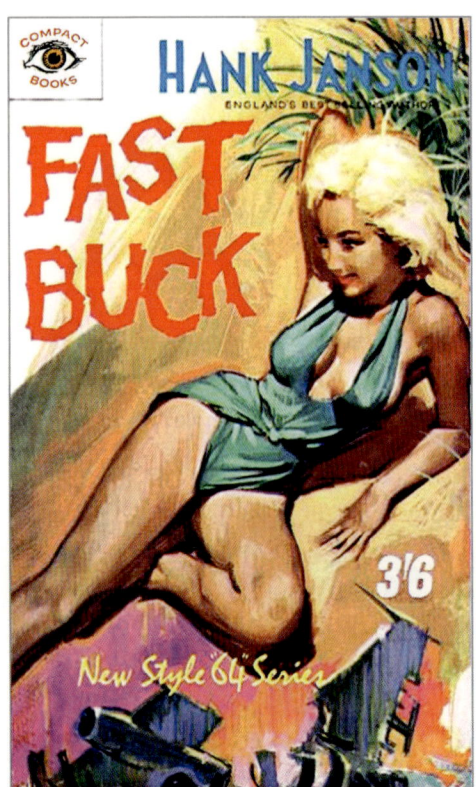

Fast Buck (1963).

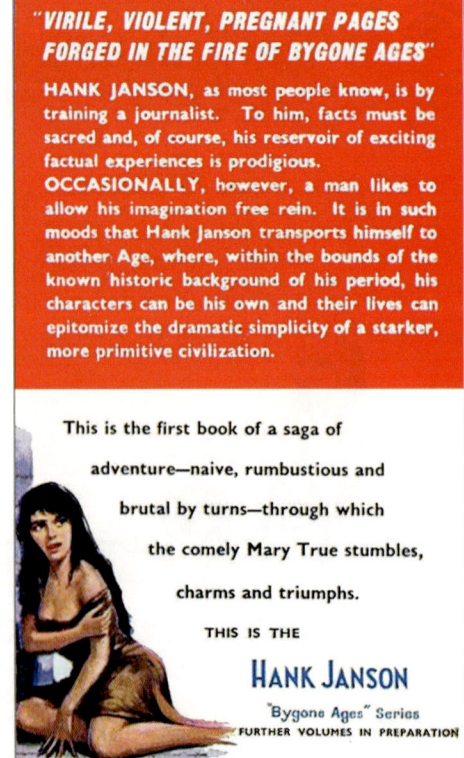

The front and back covers of the Stephen Frances-authored historical escapade *Daughter of Shame* (1963).

Hot Line (1963). Art by Michel Atkinson.

Playgirl (1963).

V for Vitality (1963). Art by Noiquet.

Visit from a Broad (1963). Art by Michel Atkinson.

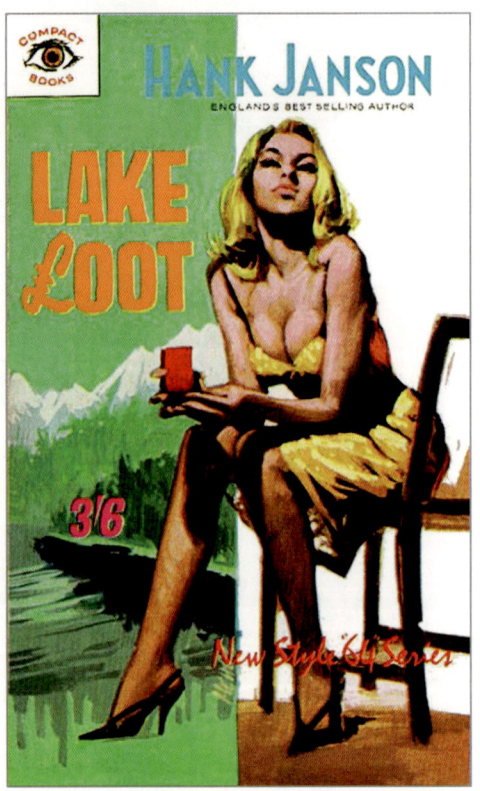
Lake Loot (1964).

Above left: with the sole exception of the historical novel *Daughter of Shame*, all of the early Compact titles up to and including *Visit from a Broad* had this generic 'Press Conference' back-cover blurb, similar in layout to the previous one (see page 158).

Above right: starting with the first 1964-published title, *Lake Loot*, a new back cover design was introduced: the top section now presented a blurb specific to the novel itself, with a monochrome detail of the front-cover art, all against a yellow background; the bottom section, which stayed the same for every book, had a short piece of text about Hank Janson, against a red background.

Bottom right: a typical early Compact-era title page

Below: the Compact imprint's initial graphic eye logo.

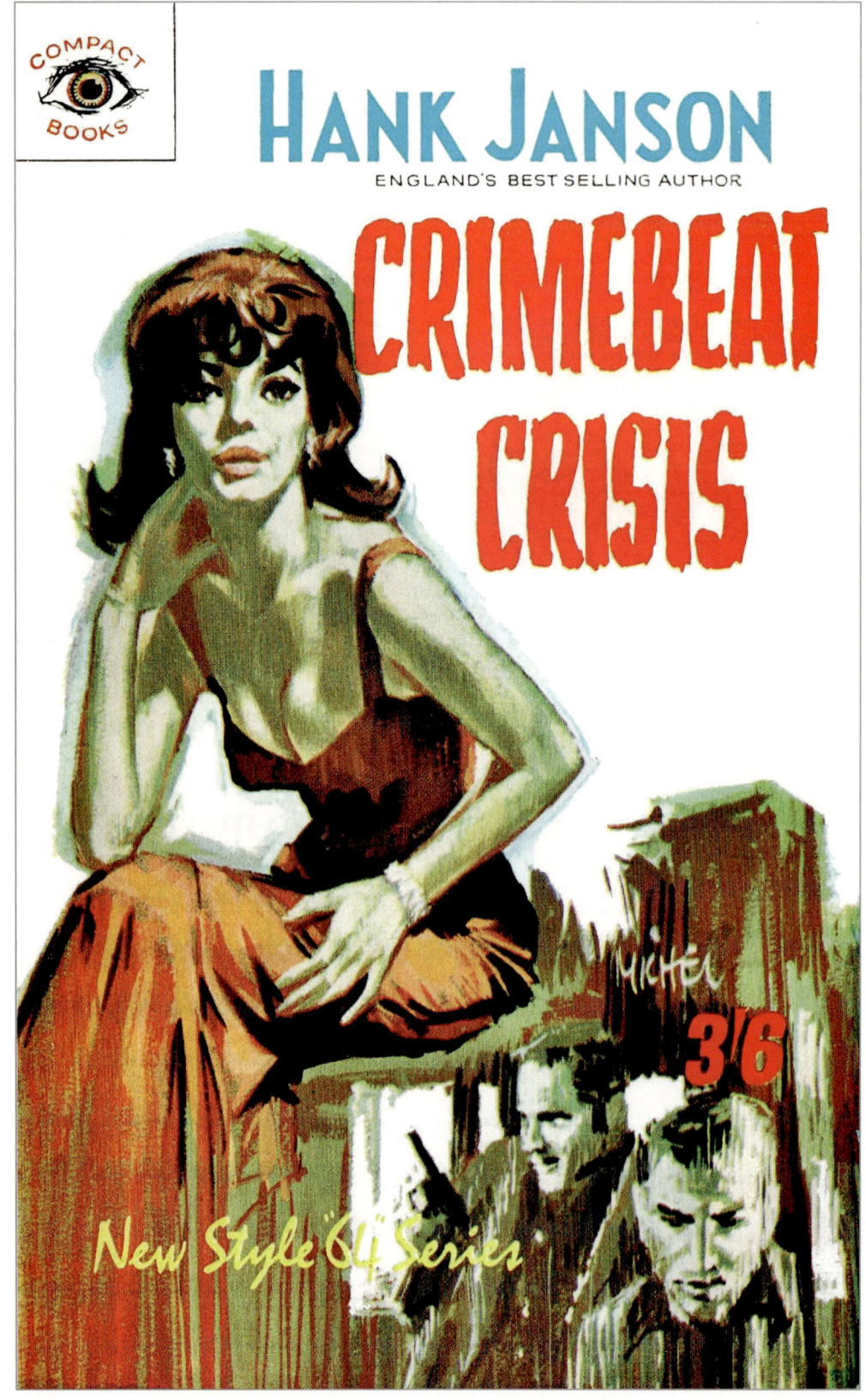

Crimebeat Crisis (1964). Art by Michel Atkinson.

Flower of Desire (1964).

Fan Fare (1964). Art by Noiquet.

TROUBLE-SHOOTER AT LARGE IN AN ALIEN LAND...
TWO SLANT-EYED CUTIES—his only hope of freedom when events take a desperate turn. HANK JANSON, seeking the truth in the depths of Red China, is tracked down and imprisoned by relentless authority. Imagine the joy and relief of being snatched from the despair of a labour camp straight into the arms of not one, but a pair of lovely oriental rescuers. But that, of course, is Hank Janson all over!

HANK JANSON'S personal experiences in straight crime-reporting, big-scale international assignments and sheer good, hard living provide an endless fund of virile stories. His prodigious energy and lively mind have combined to produce one of the most prolific and wide-ranging thriller writers of the age.

WHAT GIVES?
IDOL OF A MILLION BEAT FANS, GENE PRINCE, top disc jockey for Epic Productions, Los Angeles, had a bigger fan-mail than many of the pop stars it was his job to plug. Yet when HANK JANSON gets the tip-off from an old friend, it transpires that "The Prince" has the sort of relationship with some of his young admirers that bears a lot of investigation. Just how easy it is for a hero-worshipped figure to abuse the idolatry which is thrust upon him, and how hard it is for a decent citizen, even of Janson's persistent calibre, to expose his abuses is the pivot of a tensely exciting story.

HANK JANSON'S personal experiences in straight crime-reporting, big-scale international assignments and sheer good, hard living provide an endless fund of virile stories. His prodigious energy and lively mind have combined to produce one of the most prolific and wide-ranging thriller writers of the age.

Above: *Voodoo Violence* (1964). Art by Michel Atkinson. By this point, the novels routinely had Hank operating outside of the USA, reporting on international stories in places such as Europe, Japan and, in this instance, Haiti.

Other images on this page: four further examples of the new-style back covers introduced at the beginning of 1964. Clockwise from top right: *Flower of Desire*, *Fan Fare*, *Voodoo Violence* and *Will-Power*.

SUBVERSION BY HYPNOSIS
WHEN IT COMES TO LIGHT that an experienced and trusted secret agent has gone berserk through the mysterious influence of an expert hypnotist and his lovely raven-haired accomplice, it has to be HANK JANSON who is called in to help track down this subversive pair, and incidentally to help save the life and career of the unfortunate agent, who happened to be a pal from his Korea days. Such was the evil power of his adversary, that even Hank's reinforced-steel will-power is soon in mortal danger of succumbing and betraying his mission and his assumed identity. When, despite his efforts, he is found out, he is subjected to harrowing experiences and comes as near to violent death as he has ever been. Rescued by a brawny boatman and his attractive daughter, they join forces to beat a succession of hazards, and at last deliver the nation of one of its most dangerous menaces.

HANK JANSON'S personal experiences in straight crime-reporting, big-scale international assignments and sheer good, hard living provide an endless fund of virile stories. His prodigious energy and lively mind have combined to produce one of the most prolific and wide-ranging thriller writers of the age.

TELEPATHY? WITCHCRAFT? MAGIC?
TO THIS DAY, HANK JANSON cannot clearly define the sinister influence that overtook him and an uninvited but attractive companion in the dark island where voodoo is an everyday experience. The fate the girl suffered, and which all but embroiled the tough newshound himself, were proof enough that these horrific pagan rituals still wield an uncanny supernatural power.

HANK JANSON'S personal experiences in straight crime-reporting, big-scale international assignments and sheer good, hard living provide an endless fund of virile stories. His prodigious energy and lively mind have combined to produce one of the most prolific and wide-ranging thriller writers of the age.

Top Ten (1964). Art by Michel Atkinson.

Will-Power (1964). Art by Michel Atkinson.

Tigress (1964).

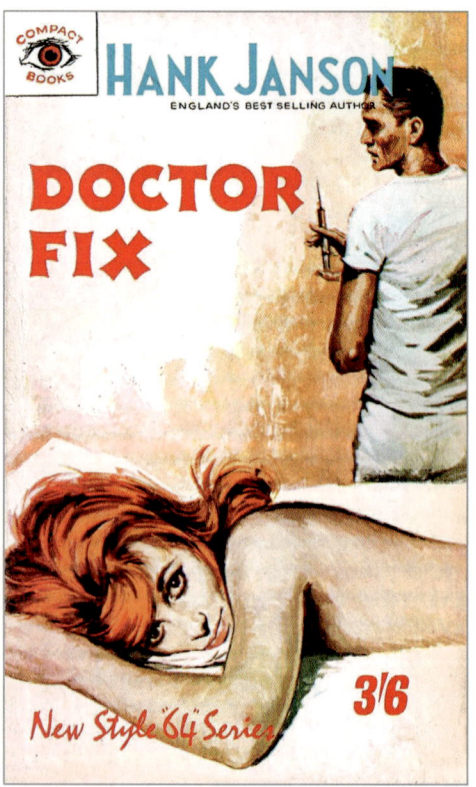
Doctor Fix (1964).

Soft Cargo (1964). Art by Michel Atkinson.

Design for Dupes (1964). Art by Michel Atkinson.

Pattern of Rape (1964). Art by Michel Atkinson.

Depravity (1964). Art by Rafael Cortiella.

That Brain Again (1964). Art by Michel Atkinson.

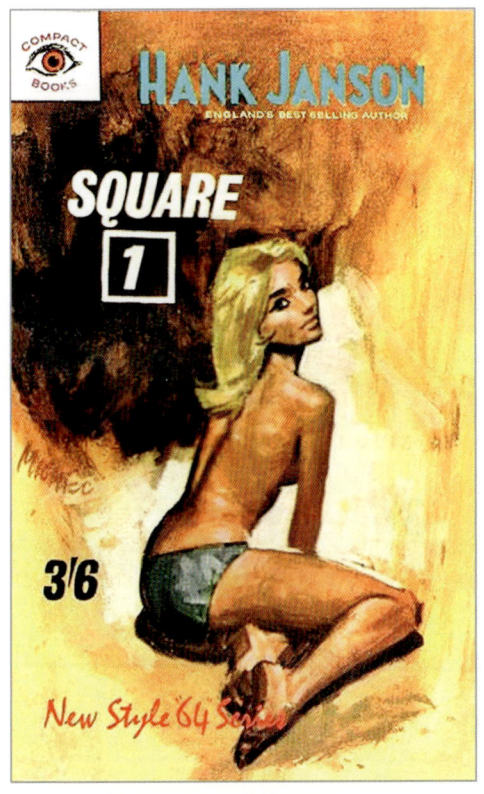
Square 1 (1964). Art by Michel Atkinson.

The Dish Ran Away (1964).

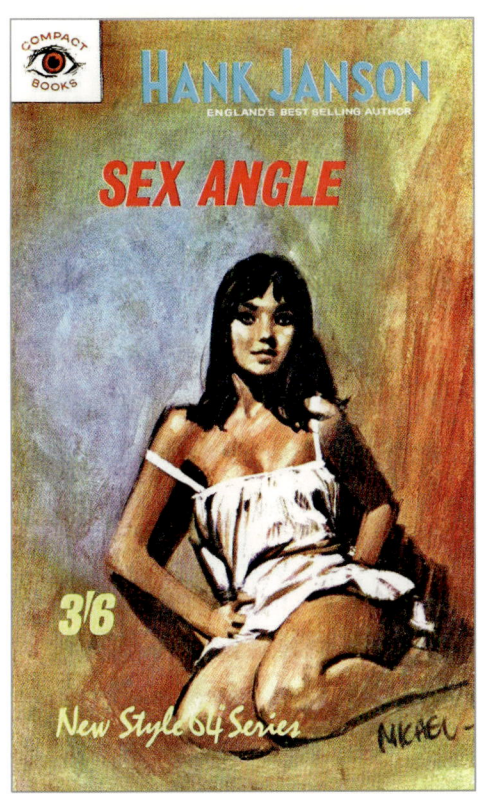
Sex Angle (1964). Art by Michel Atkinson.

The Last Lady (1964). Art by Michel Atkinson.

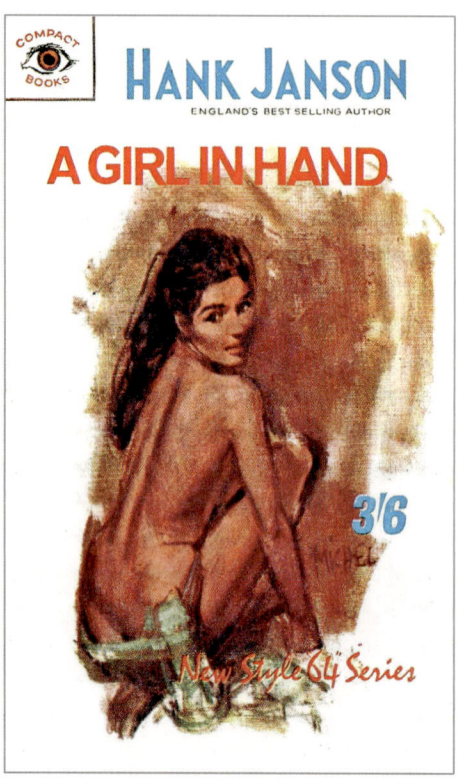

A Girl In Hand (1964). Art by Michel Atkinson.
(Image courtesy Steve Chibnall.)

The Love Secretaries (1964). Art by Michel Atkinson.

Double Take (1964). Art by Michel Atkinson.

Limbo Lover (1964). Art by Michel Atkinson.

TIGRESS!

NO DOUBT ABOUT IT, she had the measure of the big lover... and used her claws to make sure he kept his distance.
But quite a lot happens to HANK JANSON before he meets this particular match, and that includes plenty of the sort of treatment which, on balance, more than compensates for the odd let-down by a calculating fur-clad Bolivian she-cat. It was, in fact, a special personal investigation into a spot of trouble in the remote South American republic which led Hank into more difficulties than even he anticipated, and this was maybe not his most successful mission, news-wise. All the same, it adds up to a very exciting story.

HANK JANSON'S personal experiences in straight crime-reporting, big-scale international assignments and sheer good, hard living provide an endless fund of virile stories.
His prodigious energy and lively mind have combined to produce one of the most prolific and wide-ranging thriller writers of the age.

CONSPIRACY TO KILL...

A MAN OF HANK JANSON'S CAREFREE TEMPERAMENT would not normally be happy to describe himself as a student of necrology. But this in fact was what he was called upon to become when a lawyer friend drew his attention to a remarkable series of sudden deaths from "natural causes" among the richest members of the community. When a lovely redhead is enmeshed in the intrigue and the activities of the sinister "Dr. Fix" begin to come to light, Hank and his dour F.B.I. friend Max Schmidt have the necessary material for a grisly practical study of death—by design.

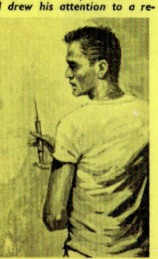

HANK JANSON'S personal experiences in straight crime-reporting, big-scale international assignments and sheer good, hard living provide an endless fund of virile stories.
His prodigious energy and lively mind have combined to produce one of the most prolific and wide-ranging thriller writers of the age.

PSYCHOPATH

THERE WAS SOMETHING UNCANNY about the latest series of murders which were making the Chicago headlines. The victims were all similar-looking blondes and their mutilated bodies were all left by their maniac-murderer with the same gruesome trademark round their strangled necks... a band of pink elastic! The pattern which Hank Janson discloses uncovers a trail of treason and deception going back to the days of the conquest of Berlin and enables a "lost" war criminal to be exposed and brought to justice.

HANK JANSON'S personal experiences in straight crime-reporting, big-scale international assignments and sheer good, hard living provide an endless fund of virile stories.
His prodigious energy and lively mind have combined to produce one of the most prolific and wide-ranging thriller writers of the age.

QUEST FOR BOOTY

SOMETHING OF THE FLAVOUR of the old-time smugglers' yarns pervades this fast-moving tale, following up a very plausible sequel to one of Britain's most famous recent crimes. The prospect of a cool few hundreds of thousands of pounds-worth of treasure-trove and the nasty death of an old friend from the old country are quite enough to get Hank Janson winging across to England, and following a pair of old arch-enemies down to a high-powered climax in the true smugglers' tradition.

HANK JANSON'S personal experiences in straight crime-reporting, big-scale international assignments and sheer good, hard living provide an endless fund of virile stories.
His prodigious energy and lively mind have combined to produce one of the most prolific and wide-ranging thriller writers of the age.

NARCOTICS

IT SEEMS THERE'S NO HONOUR among thieves when dope is at stake, and even the supposedly all-powerful "Organization" is willing to risk trying on a double-deal with Hank Janson when they find their supplies of the stuff are in peril. Never the man to miss a chance of an inside story, Hank goes in with his head down and his eyes wide open, only to find that the intrigue is a three-sided one. In mortal danger from two sets of gangsters and the subversive agents of an Eastern power, he contrives at last to break up the three interlocking rings. But it sure is a very, very near thing.

HANK JANSON'S personal experiences in straight crime-reporting, big-scale international assignments and sheer good, hard living provide an endless fund of virile stories.
His prodigious energy and lively mind have combined to produce one of the most prolific and wide-ranging thriller writers of the age.

BLANK SPOT

THERE WAS THIS UNSOLVED MYSTERY about the man's past—four days adrift from the U.N. lines in the Korean war—to which all questioning and enquiries led back. To several people, Hank Janson included, this incident appeared to have more significance than the battered wreck of what had been Matt Palmer, secret agent returned from Russian captivity would appear to justify. Yet every avenue explored in search of the truth seemed to lead back to the same blank spot—back to Square One, in fact. Fortunately there was one worth-while clue, and she was blonde, shapely and fun-loving, as Hank lost no time in discovering. She was quite delicious—right to the bitter end.

HANK JANSON'S personal experiences in straight crime-reporting, big-scale international assignments and sheer good, hard living provide an endless fund of virile stories.
His prodigious energy and lively mind have combined to produce one of the most prolific and wide-ranging thriller writers of the age.

CLOTHES MAKE THE MAN

RUNS THE ADAGE, but Lottie Kelso had her own theory that it applied equally to women, and she had one of the classiest call-houses in Chicago to prove it. She knew what seductive dressing could mean in terms of business. Trouble came when a cute little farm-girl, starry-eyed for the city lights, was picked up and brought along to swell the reserve of talented honies at Madame Kelso's establishment. She was a dish, but unfortunately she turned out also to be Lottie's own daughter! Hank Janson's friend in the vice squad put him on the scent when the dish concerned ran away and seemingly got lost. Getting her back was quite something, even for Hank.

HANK JANSON'S personal experiences in straight crime-reporting, big-scale international assignments and sheer good, hard living provide an endless fund of virile stories.
His prodigious energy and lively mind have combined to produce one of the most prolific and wide-ranging thriller writers of the age.

SUBVERSION ON THE RANGE

THE TRAGIC EVENT which blackened the name of Dallas, Texas not long ago has left in its wake a trail of speculation and unanswered questions about possible motives. Pressed, none too willingly, to follow through a lead which seemed to associate the unexplained abduction of sundry layabouts with one of the big names of Texas millionaire society, Hank Janson discovers there is much more at stake than anyone had imagined. Trouble awaits him at Broken D range, where his assumed identity is quickly discovered and his attraction to real women-folk proves a deadly embarrassment. The sinister purpose of the mystery range becomes apparent, but a pitched gun-battle has to be fought before the power behind it all can be revealed. Then the full horror and significance of what had gone before—and what might have happened but for Hank's intervention—is dramatically exposed.

HANK JANSON'S personal experiences in straight crime-reporting, big-scale international assignments and sheer good, hard living provide an endless fund of virile stories.
His prodigious energy and lively mind have combined to produce one of the most prolific and wide-ranging thriller writers of the age.

KIDNAPPING

TO ATTACK A man through his son is a vile form of revenge. And when that son is on the other side of the Atlantic, one can sympathise even more with his parents' fears for his safety. Hank Janson is called in to protect the boy, and finds himself embroiled in the life and intrigues of an English Public School—to say nothing of a certain "old boy" who is determined to make his stay as uncomfortable and painful as possible. His unwelcome attentions, plus the threat to the boy keep Hank busy enough, but not too busy to ignore the local innkeeper's daughter, who offers him not only her help, but also certain extra-mural activities not included in the school curriculum.

HANK JANSON'S personal experiences in straight crime-reporting, big-scale international assignments and sheer good, hard living provide an endless fund of virile stories.
His prodigious energy and lively mind have combined to produce one of the most prolific and wide-ranging thriller writers of the age.

Nine further examples of the back cover design used during 1964: *Tigress, Doctor Fix, Pattern of Rape, That Brain Again, Depravity, Square 1, The Dish Ran Away, The Last Lady* and *Double Take*. The colour scheme recalls that of the Alexander Moring-era books.

The 'New Style "64" Series' having ended at the close of 1964, 1965 saw the Hank Janson range undergo a change of regular cover design. The Compact logo and author credit were both revamped, but more significantly, the previous approach of featuring full-page front cover artwork was dropped in favour of the simpler – and doubtless cheaper – idea of having simply a small vignette, generally in a rather muted colour palette, placed against a white background, along with a short piece of 'teaser' text. The result was a run of covers that, sadly, were far less striking and attractive than those that had come before. The back covers continued to present a monochrome detail of the front cover artwork, but instead of the previous red-and-yellow colour scheme, the top section was now in white, and the bottom section in a colour that changed for each book – usually matching the colour of the front cover title lettering.

Top left and bottom right: the front and back covers of the first 1965 title, *Jazz Jungle*. Top right: a detail of the front cover artwork vignette for *Jazz Jungle*.

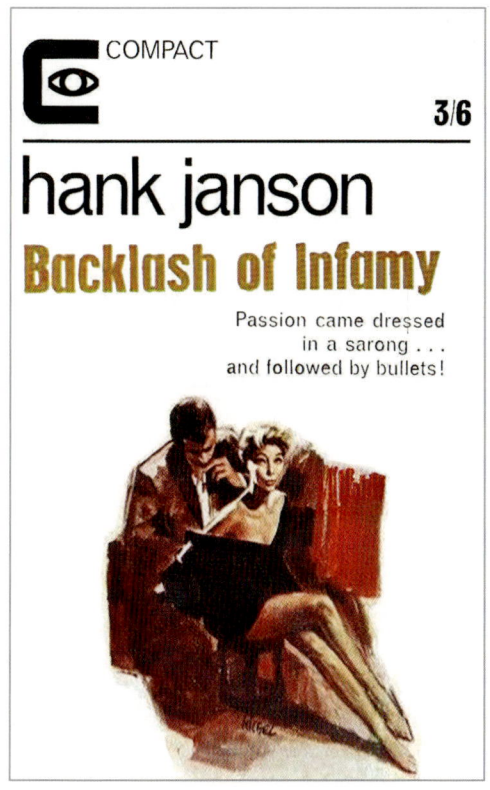
Backlash of Infamy (1965). Art by Michel Atkinson.

Counter-Feat (1965). Art by Michel Atkinson.

Model in Mayhem (1965). Art by Louis Shabner.

Berlin Briefing (1965). Art by Michel Atkinson.

Lust for Vengeance (1965). Art by Michel Atkinson.

Say It With Candy (1965).

Sweet Talk (1965). Art by Louis Shabner.

Missile Mob (1965).

Abomination (1965). Art by Louis Shabner.

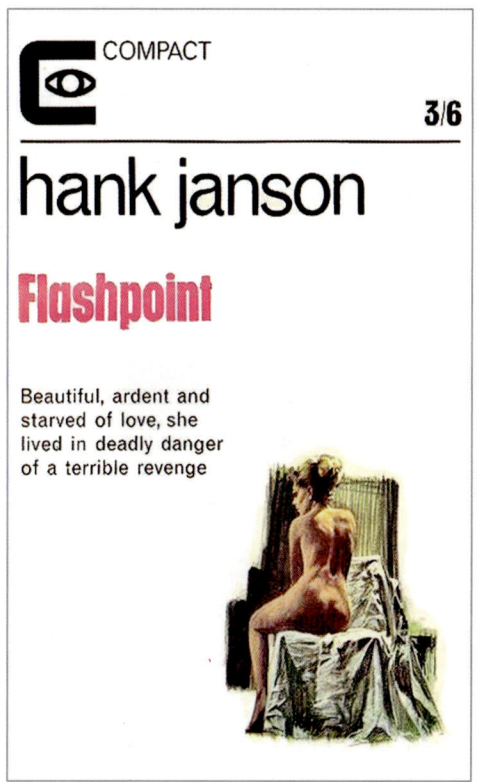

Flashpoint (1965). Art by Michel Atkinson.

Junk Market (1965). Art by Louis Shabner.

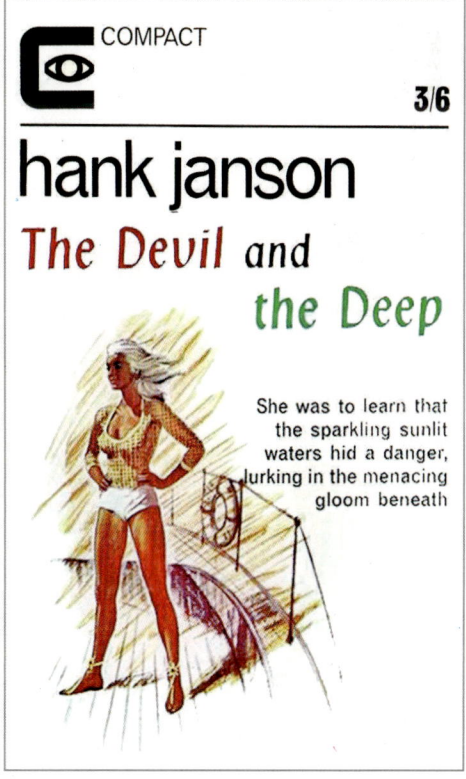

The Devil and the Deep (1965).

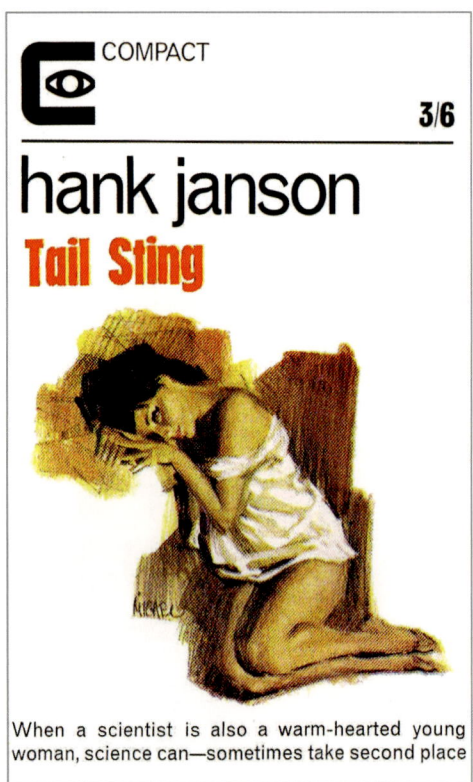

Tail Sting (1965). Art by Michel Atkinson.

Why Should Sylvia? (1965). Art by Louis Shabner.

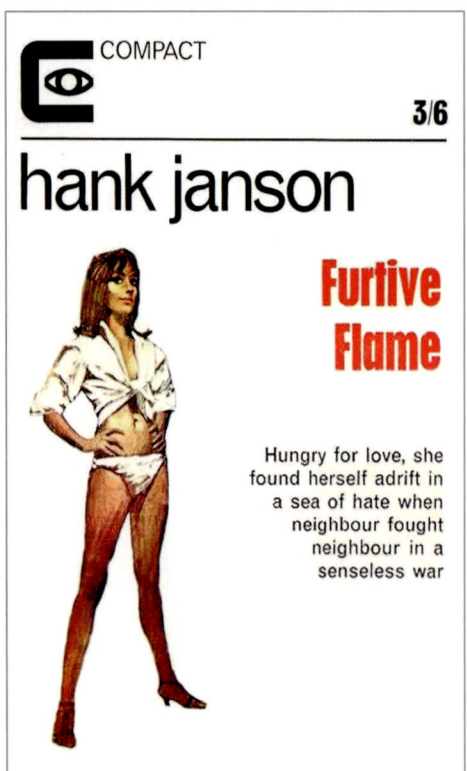

Furtive Flame (1965).

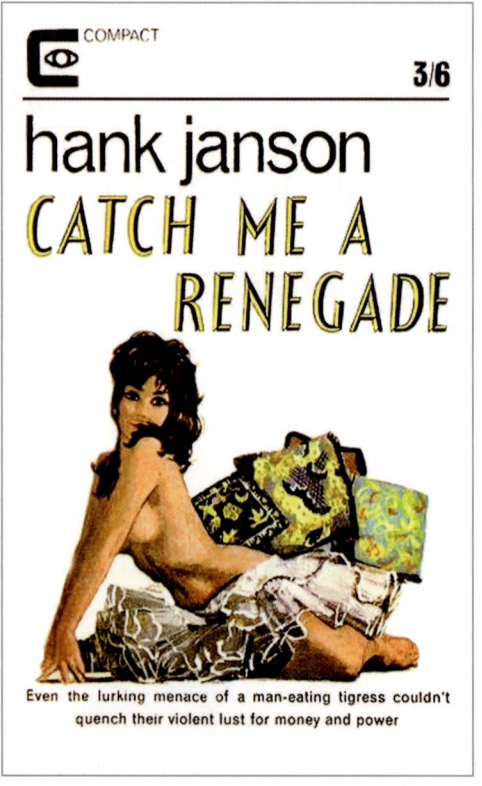

Catch Me a Renegade (1965).

Roxy by Proxy (1965).

Helldorado (1966).

Escalation (1966). (Image courtesy Steve Chibnall.)

Physical Attraction (1966).

Liquor is Quicker (1966).

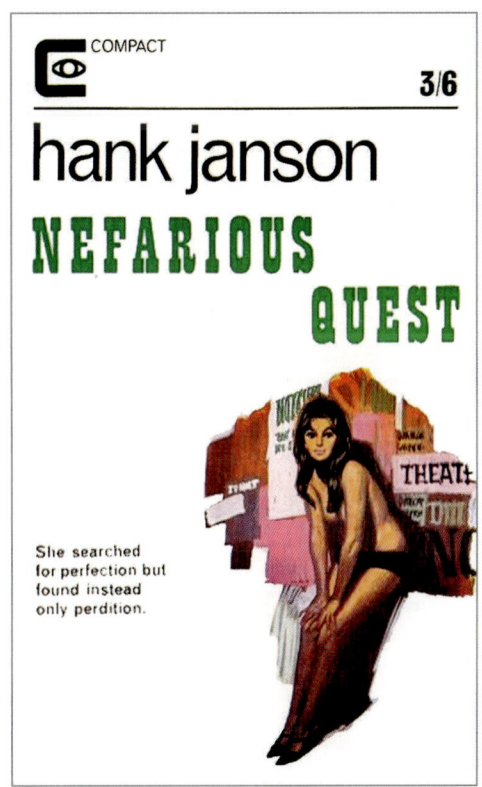
Nefarious Quest (1966).

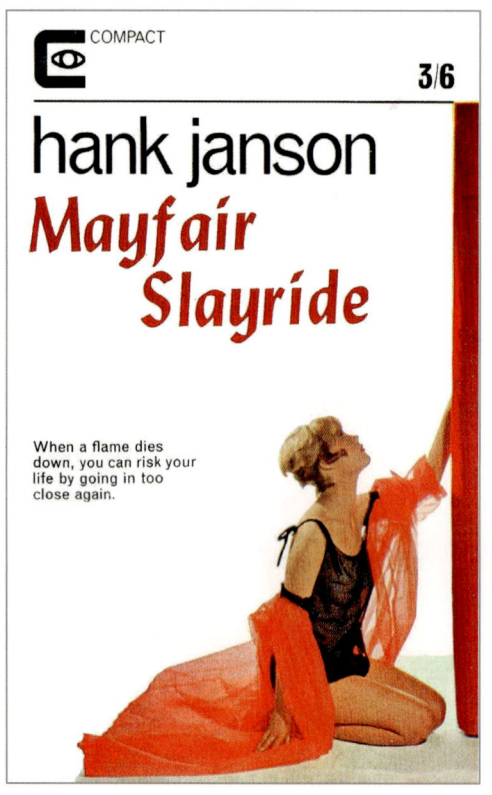

Mayfair Slayride (1966).

Krush (1966).

Dead Certainty (1966).

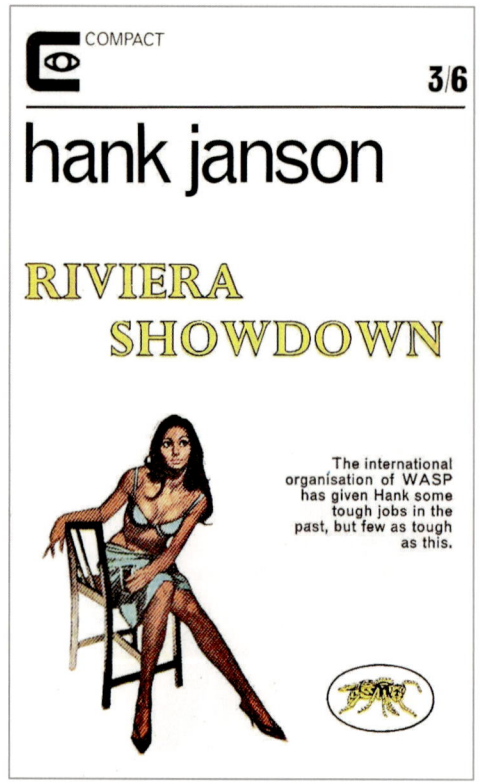

Riviera Showdown (1966).

In 1966, nine Hank Janson short stories appeared in successive issues of a new men's adult magazine, *Golden Nugget*, published by Dagg Books Ltd, one of the Gold family's Gold Star ventures. The debut issue – see top right – came out in March, and the last – centre right – in November. The first eight stories were written by one of the novels' regular authors, Jim Moffatt, the ninth was by Michael Moorcock. Each was graced by a black-and-white illustration; the one for Moorcock's story, 'The Girl Who Killed Sultry Caine', is shown immediately below. Bottom row: the covers of Issues 3, 4, 6 and 7.

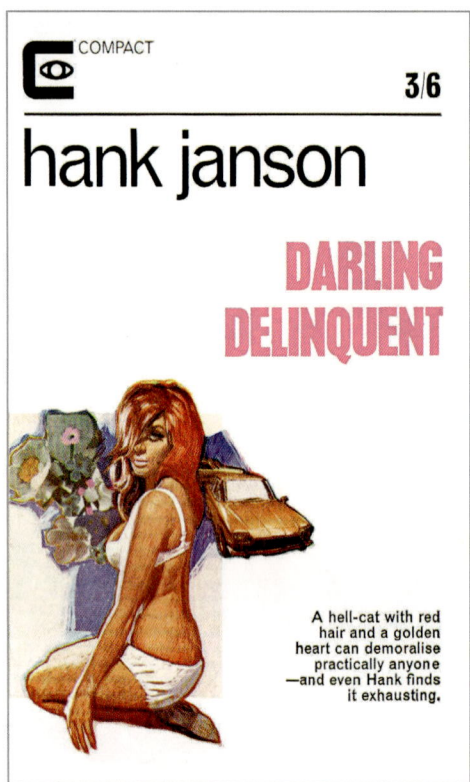
Darling Delinquent (1966).

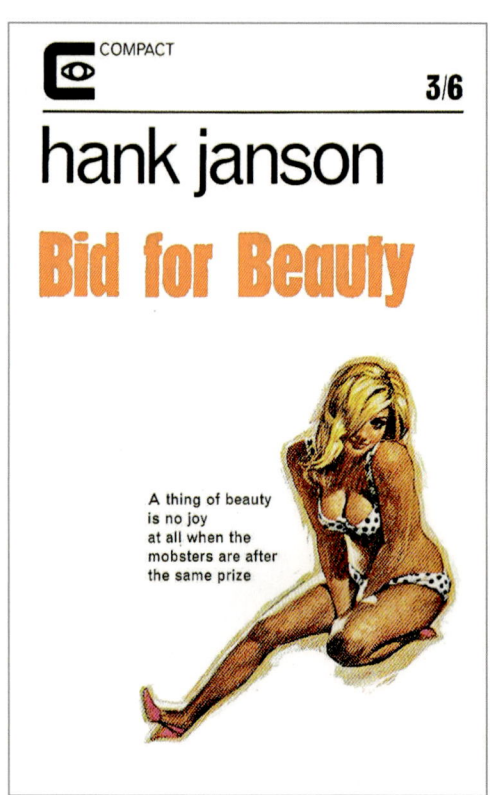
Bid for Beauty (1966).

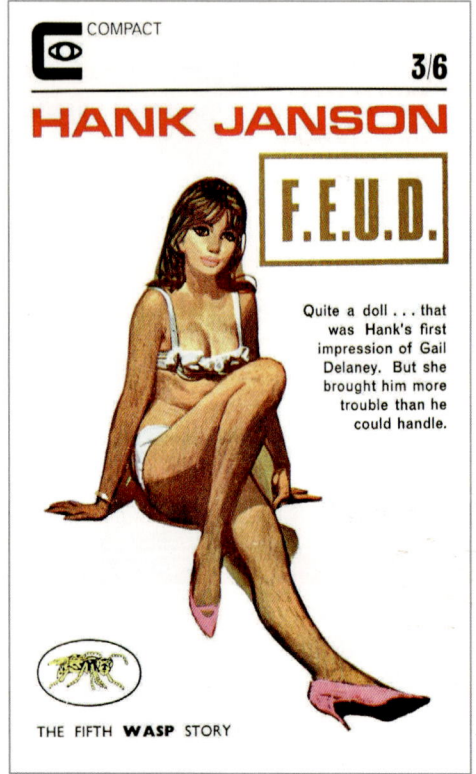
F.E.U.D. (1966).

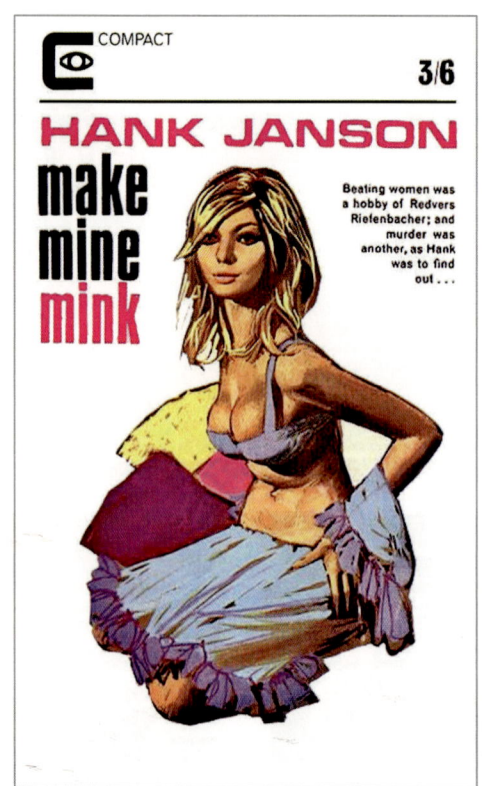
Make Mine Mink (1966).

The Big H (1967).

Ladybirds Are In (1967).

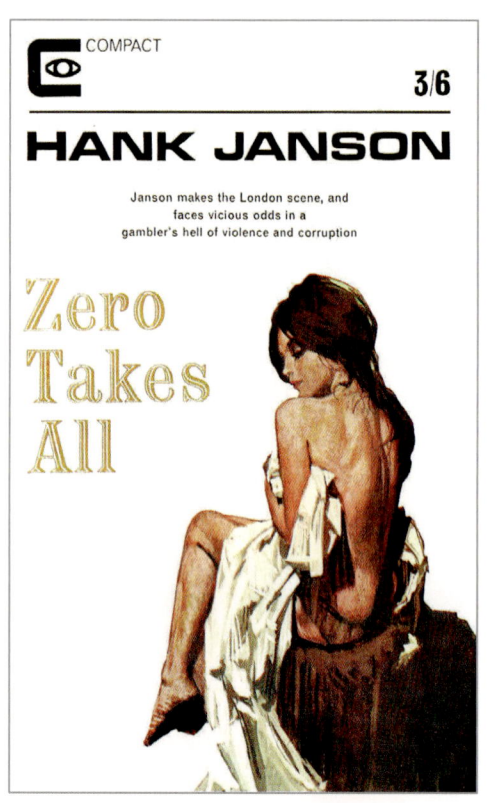
Zero Takes All (1967).

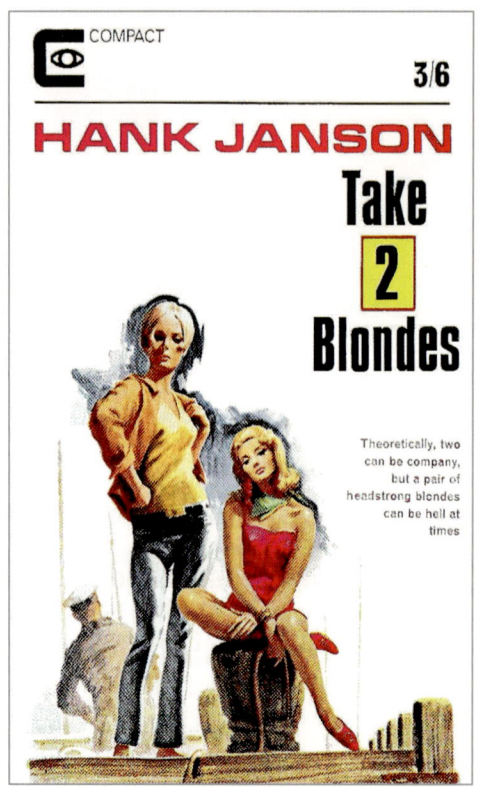
Take 2 Blondes (1967).

One-Way Split (1967). Art by Louis Shabner.

Operation Obliterate (1967). Art by Sam Peffer.

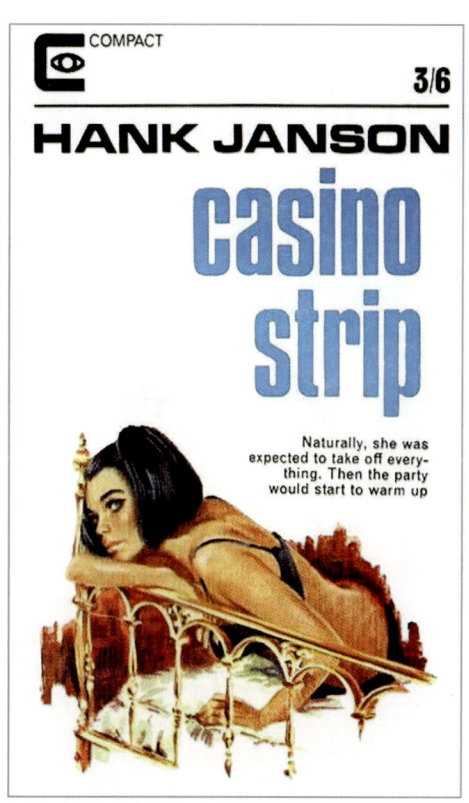
Casino Strip (1967). Art by Sam Peffer.

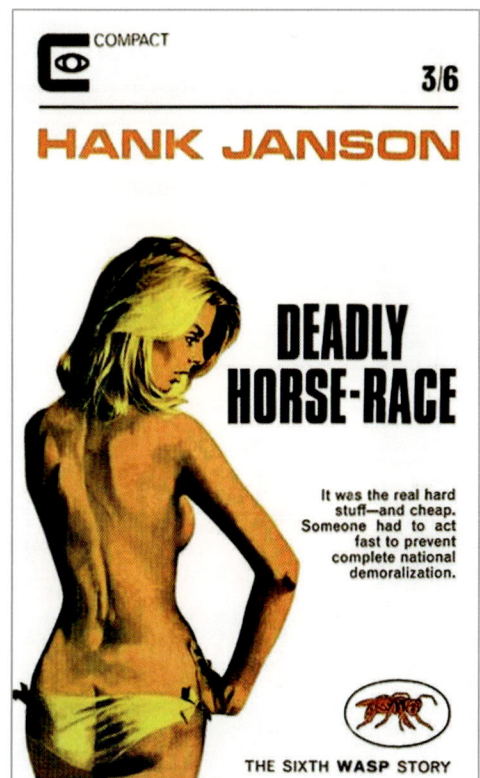
Deadly Horse-Race (1967).

Hell Brood (1967).

Casinopoly (1967).

Same Difference (1967).

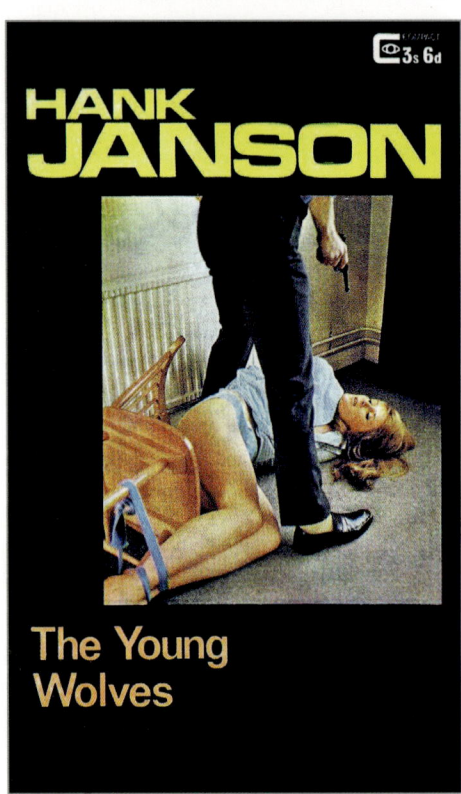

The Young Wolves (1967).

Love-In and Lamentation (1968).

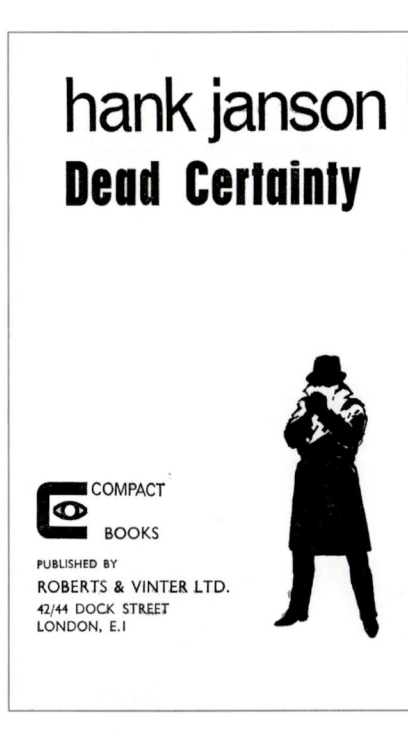  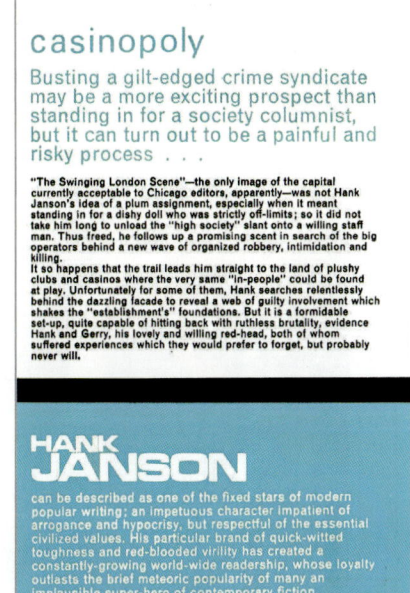

In 1966, the iconic Hank Janson silhouette logo was for the first time redesigned. The new version – see above centre – was thereafter used in place of the original both on the books' spines and on their title pages – see above left for one example. Toward the end of the following year, however, a more radical change occurred, when artwork front covers were dropped altogether in favour of – frankly terrible – photographic ones, the first four of which are reproduced opposite. These new-style covers, a world away from the beautiful artwork of Reginald Heade, were then sadly persisted with until the range's end. The books' back covers, which now claimed total worldwide sales exceeding 20,000,000, also became plainer – as evidenced by the example pictured above right, for *Casinopoly* – no longer having the benefit of being able to feature a detail of the front cover artwork – as seen in the three further examples shown below, for *Dead Certainty*, *The Big H* and *F.E.U.D.*

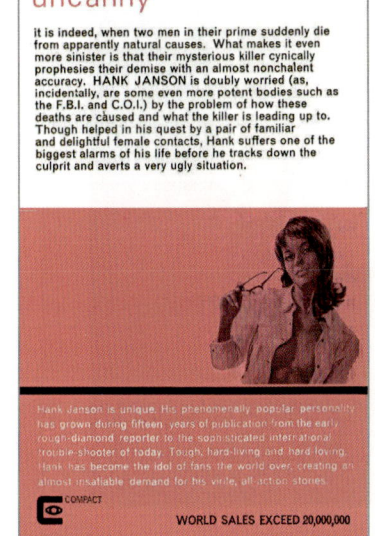 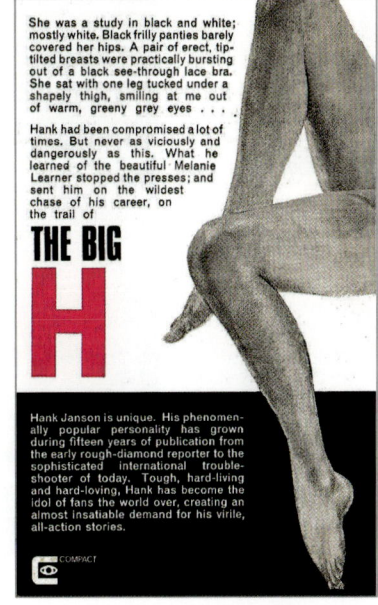 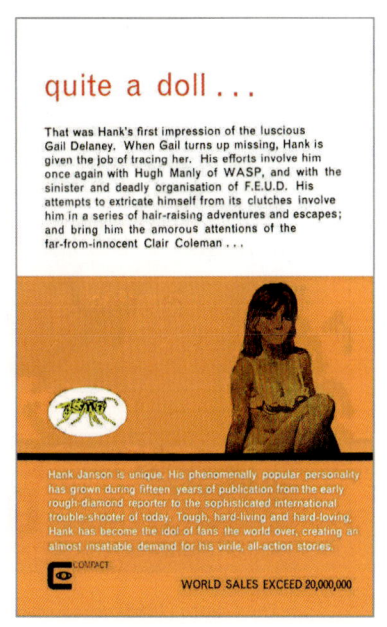

Shalom, My Love (1968).

Microkill (1968).

The Crunch (1968). (Image courtesy Steve Chibnall.)

Sprung! (1968).

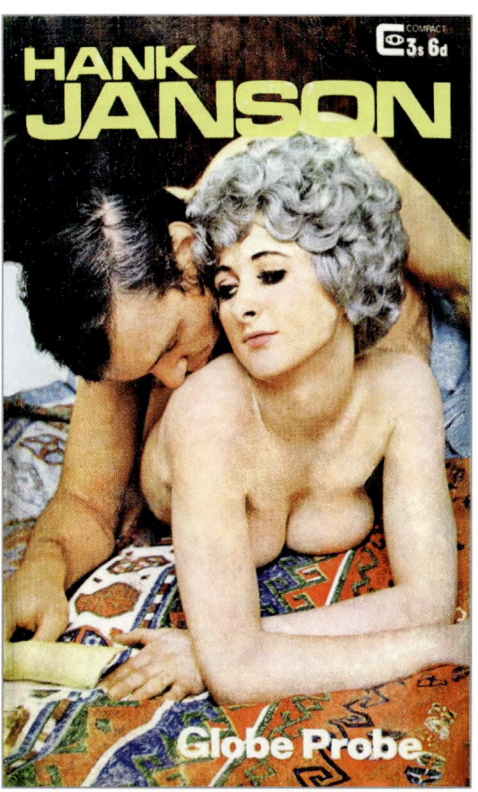

Cat's Paw (1969).   *Globe Probe* (1969).

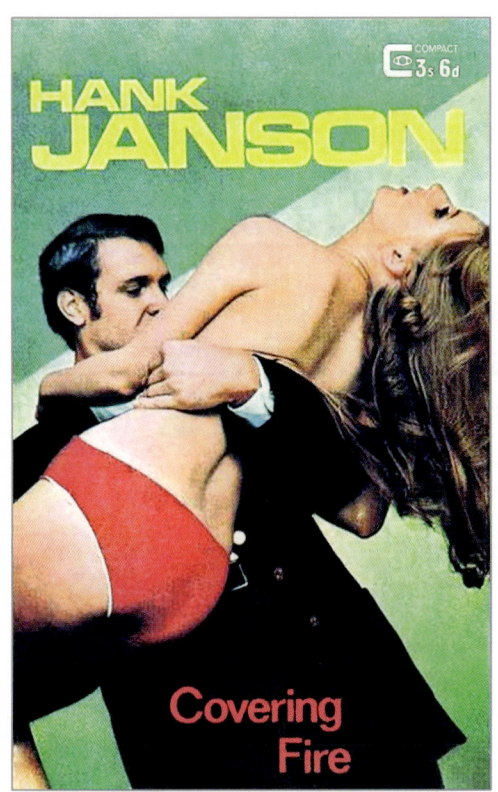
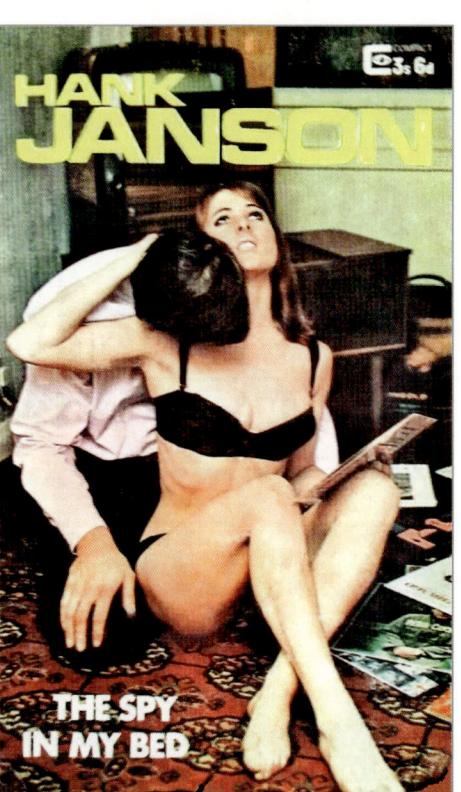

Covering Fire (1969).   *The Spy in My Bed* (1969).

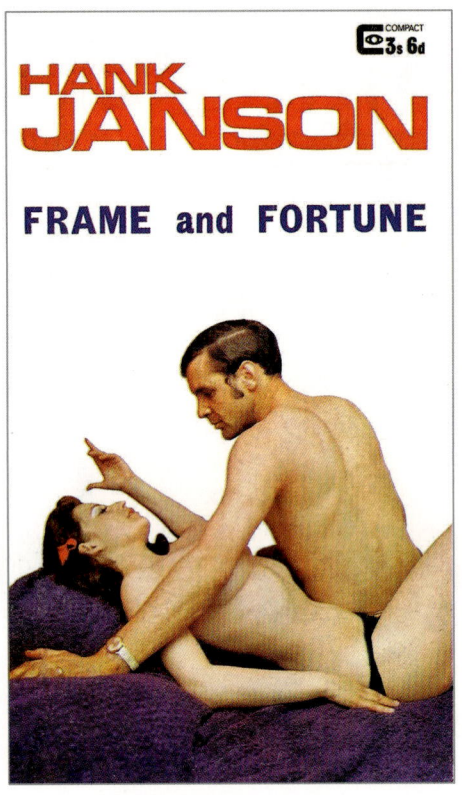

Frame and Fortune (1970).

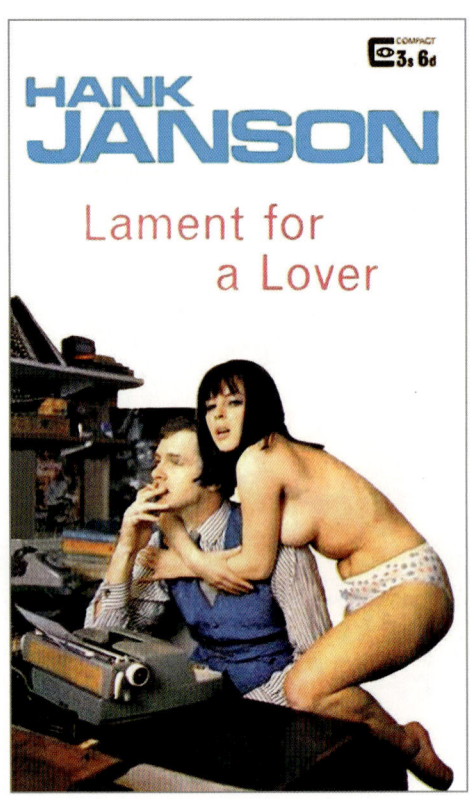

Lament for a Lover (1970).

Ultimate Deterrent (1970).

Twilight Tigress (1970).

The Big Round Bed (1970).

Infiltration (1970).

Villon of the Peace (1970).

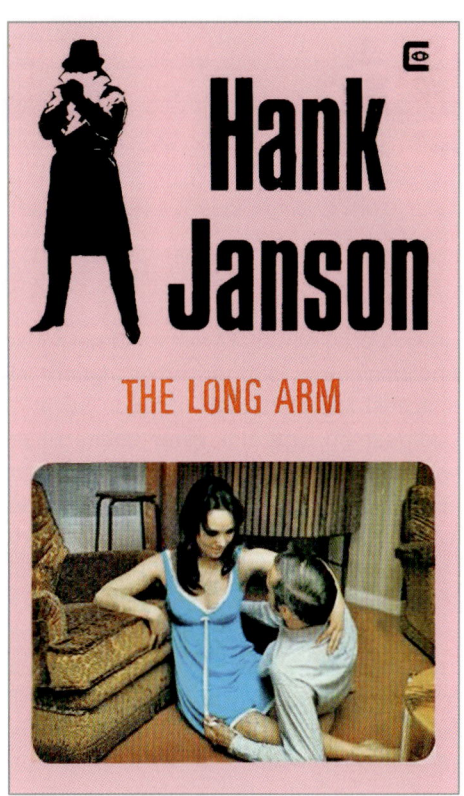

The Long Arm (1970).

The Kay Assignation (1971).

Caribbean Caper (1971).

The Liz Assignation (1971).

Grass Widow (1971).

COMPACT REISSUES

  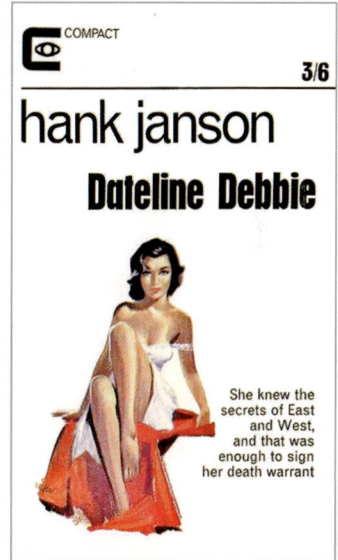

Above: three new-style reissues of earlier titles published by Roberts & Vinter under the Compact imprint. Reused art by Michel Atkinson. Atkinson also supplied most of the newly-commissioned vignettes for the reissues range, although at least one (for *Square 1*, retitled *Square One* for this edition) was provided by Louis Shabner under his 'Shel' pseudonym.

The publication of the final Gold & Warburton book, *Grass Widow*, early in 1971 brought to an end the incredible 25-year run of the original Hank Janson range. Two further titles, *The Sleeping-Beauty Case* and *Dateline – Death*, were promoted as forthcoming, but never appeared.

Since the books were redesigned at the start of 1965, not only had many new titles been published, but almost all of the earlier Compact ones, and some of the pre-Compact Roberts & Vinter ones, had been reissued, stripped of their original covers and given new-style replacements. Most of these appeared in 1966. Although it seems that the old Alexander Moring-era stock copies had finally been exhausted, some of those titles were also reprinted with new-style Compact covers. The result was a veritable glut of Hank Janson books competing for space on newsagents' shelves – which could perhaps have been one of the factors contributing to the downturn in sales of the ongoing range.

Most of the artwork vignettes used for the covers of these Compact reissues and reprints appeared on multiple titles, and – unlike those for the new novels – not all of them were specially-commissioned; some consisted simply of elements borrowed from earlier artwork. The three pictured above, for instance, took the female figures from the covers of the original editions of *Crime on My Hands*, *Honey for Me* and *Mistress of Fear* respectively (see pages 145-147). Over the next six pages are presented a representative selection of examples.

Even after Gold & Warburton's demise, the Hank Janson books remained in circulation for some time, owing in part to the unsold stock copies being bought up by fly-by-night wholesaler Knight Books, who marketed them with their own chess-piece logo stickered over the Compact one. In a few cases, Knight even went so far as to have their own replacement covers printed up and substituted – the *Visit from a Broad* and *Daughter of Shame* reissues shown in the bottom right-hand corner on page 203 are two examples of these now-scarce versions.

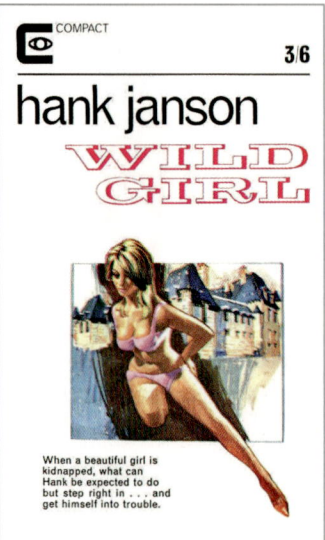

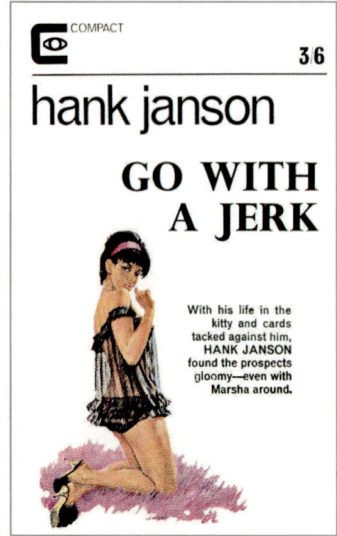

COMPACT REISSUES

hank janson — I For Intrigue — 3/6
Only luck saved her from the hell-life of a broken slave, selling her body in a vice-den

hank janson — Tigress — 3/6
Warm, soft and desirable... but she used her hidden claws to make sure he kept his distance

hank janson — Dateline Diane — 3/6
Teenage beauty queens are big news when they disappear without trace — and bigger still when Poppa is a top producer in Hollywood.

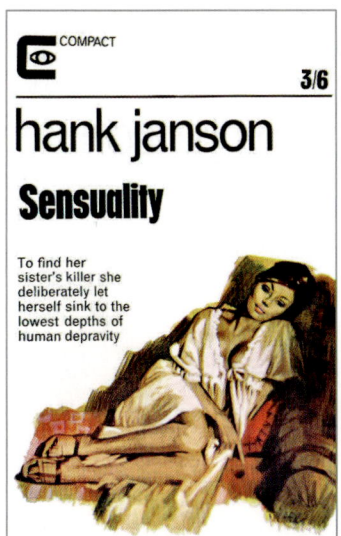

hank janson — Sensuality — 3/6
To find her sister's killer she deliberately let herself sink to the lowest depths of human depravity

hank janson — Playgirl — 3/6
Because she was rich and lovely, she was a natural for the clutching hands of evil people

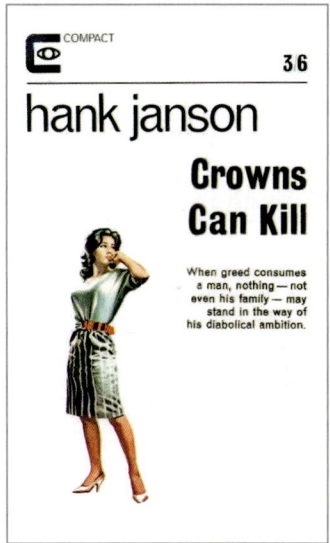

hank janson — Crowns Can Kill — 3/6
When greed consumes a man, nothing — not even his family — may stand in the way of his diabolical ambition.

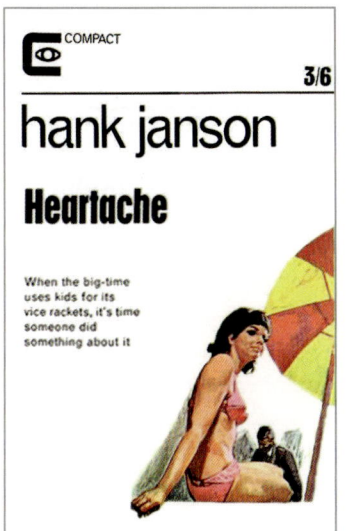

hank janson — Heartache — 3/6
When the big-time uses kids for its vice rackets, it's time someone did something about it

hank janson — Sex Angle — 3/6
Though a policeman's lot may not be a happy one, Rita helped to make it less unhappy than it might have been

hank janson — Last Lady — 3/6
Beneath her alluring body was a steely strength ready for any emergency

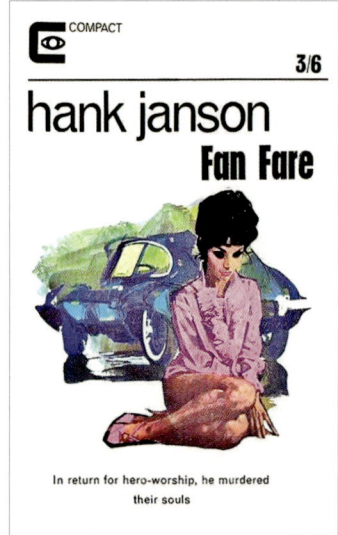
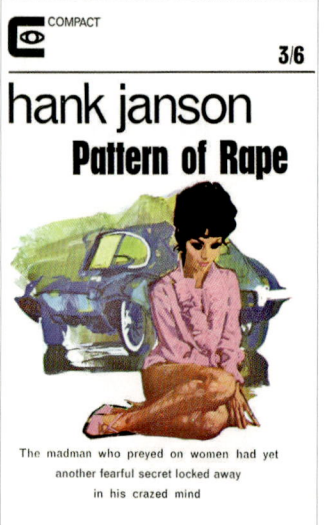

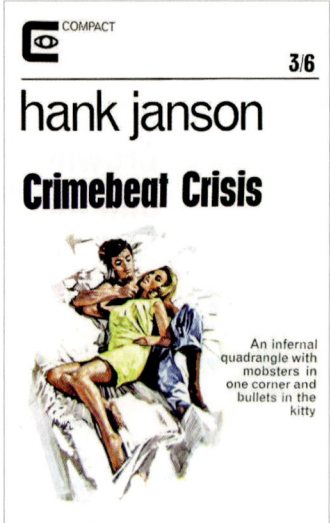
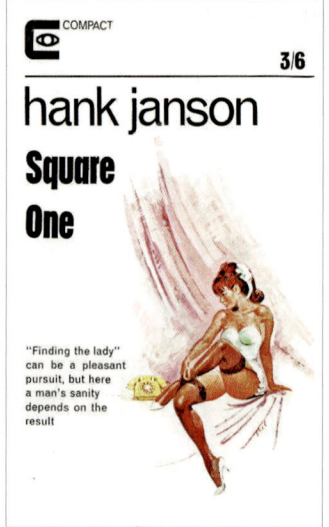

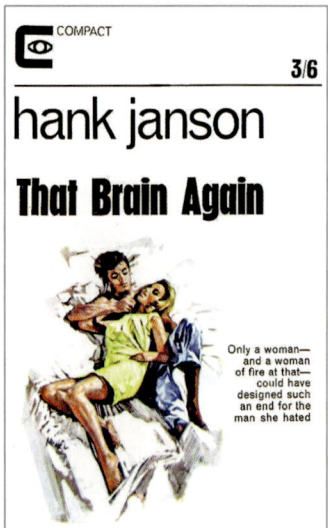

COMPACT REISSUES

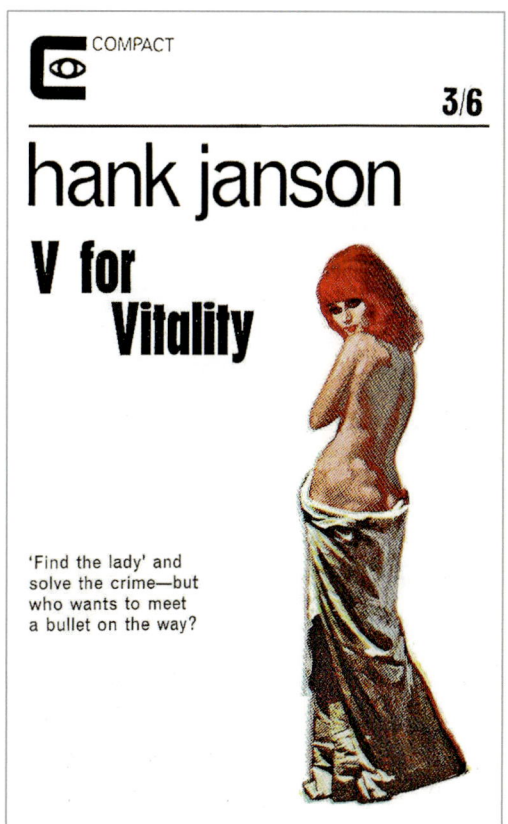

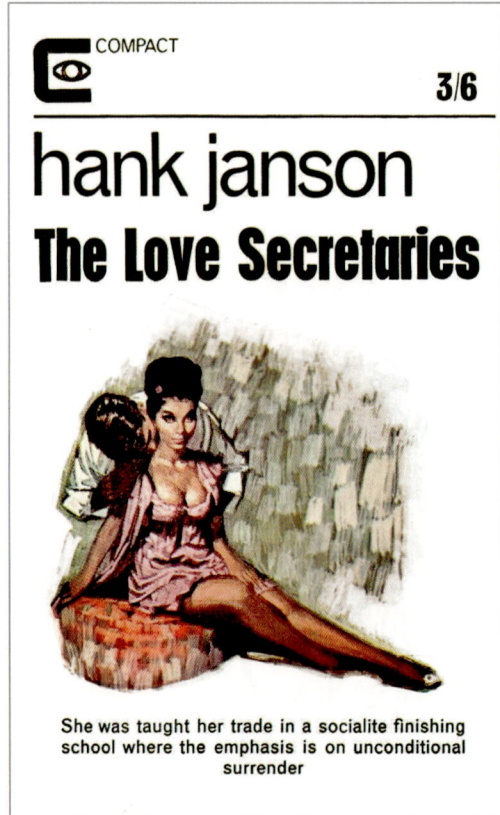

COMPACT REISSUES

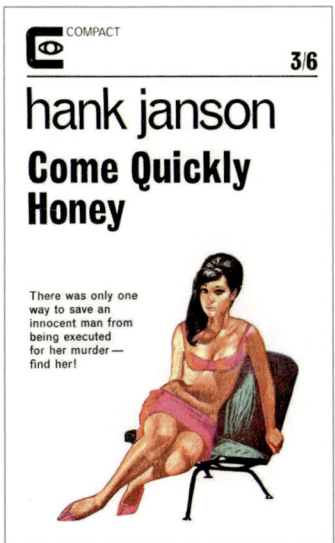
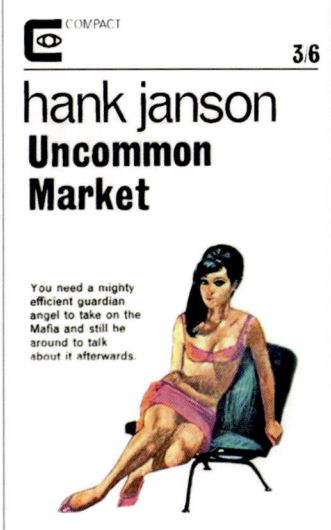
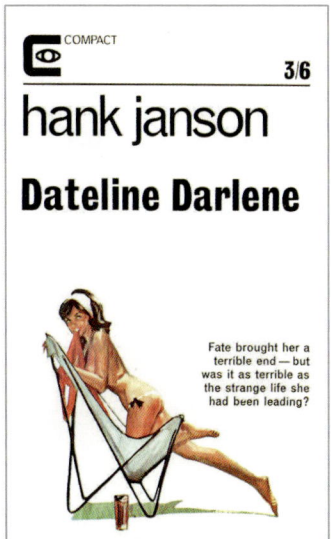
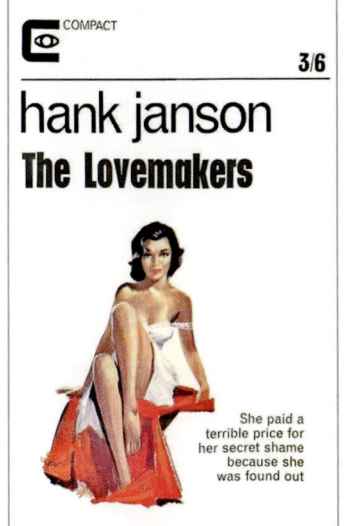
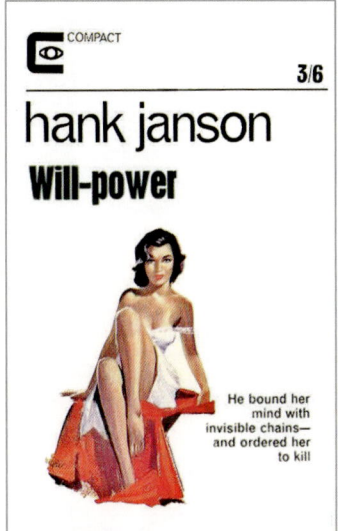
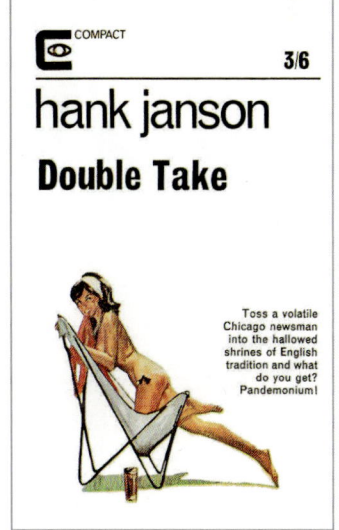

News Girl (1963), the first Hilary Brand spin-off novel. Art by Michel Atkinson.

HILARY BRAND

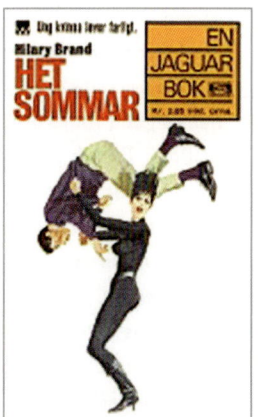

Above left: a 1966 Compact reissue of *News Girl*, with a new-style cover. Above right: Swedish translations of *Black Summer Day*, retitled *Het Sommar* (*Hot Summer*), issued by Wennerbergs Förlag in 1968 in their Jaguar series; and *Brand T*, retitled *T som i Trinidad* (*T as in Trinidad*), the same publisher's c1979 Dubbeldeckare (Double Decker) reissue of a 1970 Jaguar series entry.

Having featured in three early 1963 Hank Janson novels – *Second String*, *Brand Image* and *Hilary's Terms* – Hilary Brand then became the subject of her own spin-off range. This eventually ran to a total of eight titles, all published under Roberts & Vinter's Compact imprint at 3/6 each. These were: *News Girl* (1963), *Brand T* (1964), *Peak of Frenzy* (1964), *Black Summer Day* (1965), *All – Or Something* (1965), *A Flair for Affairs* (1966), *Strictly Wild* (1966) and finally *Running Scared* (1966). The first four were written by the character's creator, Stephen Frances, and the others by Jim Moffatt – although Michael Moorcock contributed a couple of extra chapters to *Running Scared*, as Moffatt's manuscript came in too short. All eight books are pictured in this section.

Sadly the Hilary Brand range never came close to matching the success of the Hank Janson one, although it did also spawn some foreign language editions: four Dutch – see page 209 – and two Swedish, one of which had a reissue – see above.

NEWS GIRL

Her father, the oil tycoon, vowed when his only son was killed in action that his remaining child would have everything.

By age 20 she had enjoyed a liberal and expensive education, world travel, clothes, cars and every material luxury. Native vivacity and striking auburn-haired good looks brought her a string of Palm Beach playboy suitors.

After a year or so of high life, Hilary suddenly opted for the one thing her father never thought to offer her— a career.

Starting at the bottom as a reporter on a small-time paper she chanced upon famed news-hound HANK JANSON. Studied use of persuasion and pressure soon got her an introduction to Hank's paper and a break in big-time journalism.

In NEWS GIRL she throws all the vitality of her young personality into the story of her first month's adventures as a feature writer. You'll want to go all the way along with

HILARY BRAND

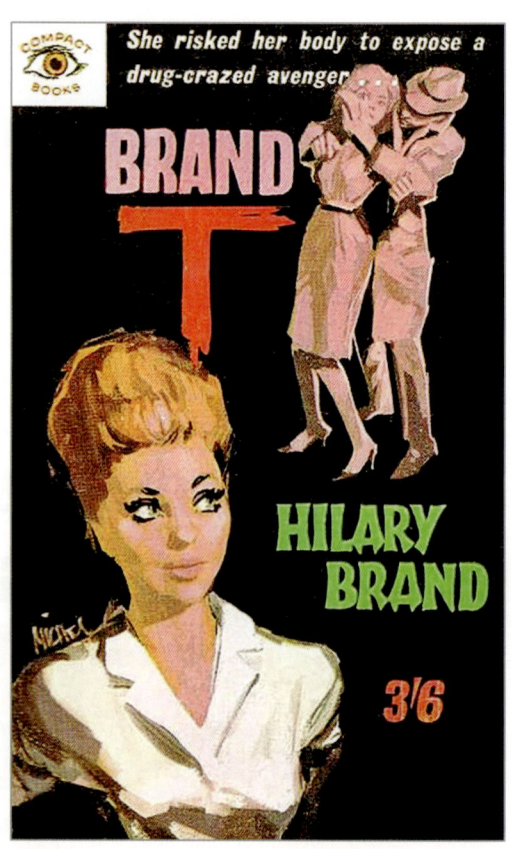

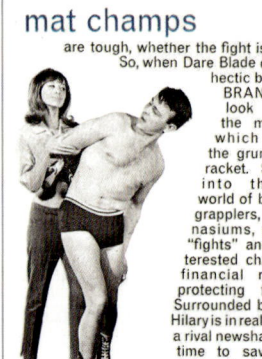

Above: the back cover of the first edition of *News Girl* gives brief details of Hilary Brand's character and explains the premise of the spin-off range.

Top right: *Brand T* (1964). Art by Michel Atkinson.

Bottom right: *Peak of Frenzy* (1964).

Left: the back cover of *All – Or Something* (1965). The Hilary Brand range's adoption of photographic covers preceded the Hank Janson's, though artwork returned for the final two books.

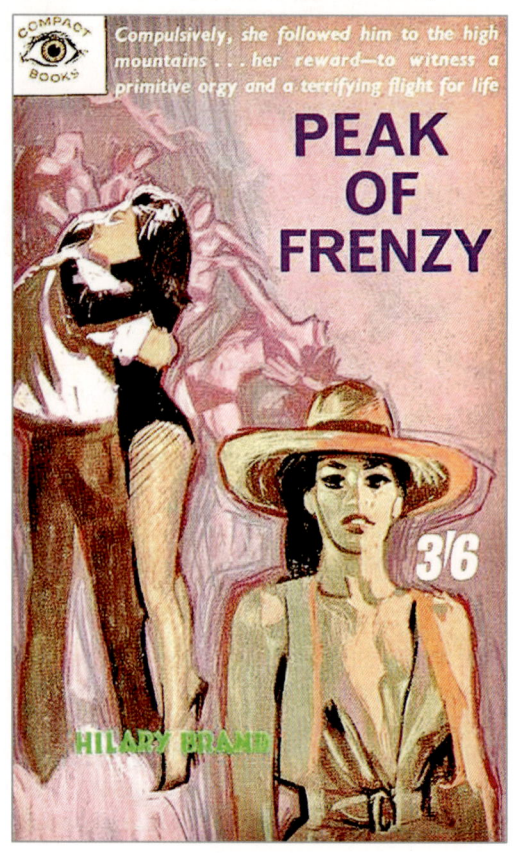

Black Summer Day (1965). Art by Michel Atkinson.

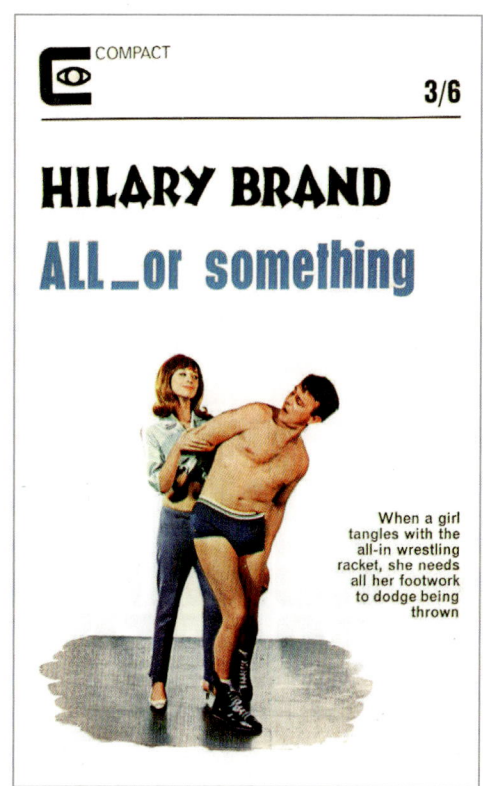

All – Or Something (1965).

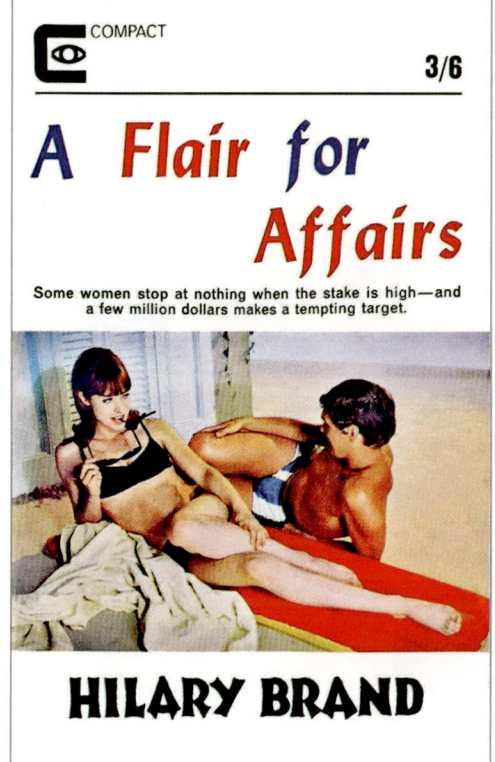

A Flair for Affairs (1966).

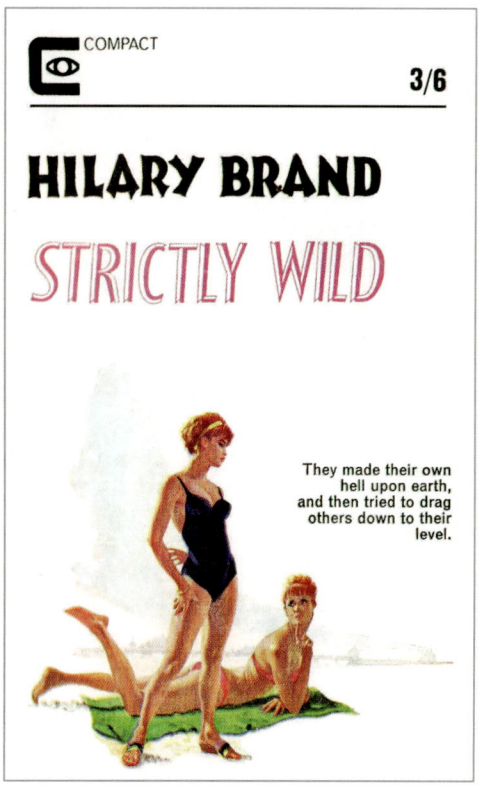

Strictly Wild (1966).

Running Scared (1966)

HILARY BRAND

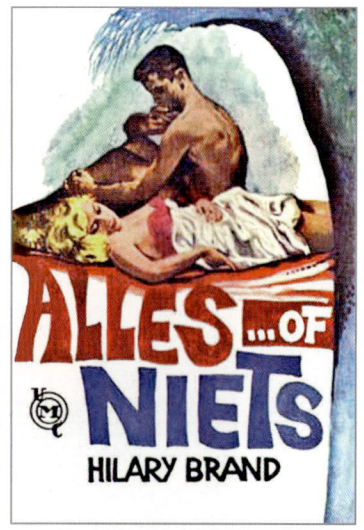

Pictured here are the four Dutch-language Hilary Brand novels, which all appeared circa 1968 from UMC – full name Uitgevers Maatschappij de Combinatie – a company that published editions of numerous British pulp crime books, mostly printed in Belgium and distributed throughout the Benelux countries. It is a moot point whether UMC really had the rights to produce these titles, or whether they were essentially illicit.

Above: *De Tijger is Los* (*The Tiger is Loose*), a translation of *Strictly Wild*.

Top right: *Alles … Of Niets* (*All … Or Nothing*), a translation of *All – Or Something*.

Centre right: *Zwardte Dagen* (*Black Days*), a translation of *Black Summer Day*.

Bottom right: *Gevoel Voor Feiten* (*Sense of Facts*), a translation of *A Flair for Affairs*. The female subject of this artwork was a copy of that featured on the cover for the Hank Janson novel *Doctor Fix* (see page 170), but flipped horizontally.

US edition of *Lady, Mind That Corpse* (Checkerbooks, 1949). Reused art by Reginald Heade, taken from the UK edition of *Honey, Take My Gun* (see page 24).

NORTH AMERICAN EDITIONS

Orchids to You (Pony, c1950).

Smart Girls Don't Talk (Flamingo, 1951)

All the Hank Janson books that Stephen Frances published during 1949 and 1950 had printed in their preliminary pages the statement, 'Rights throughout the World, except England, reserved to Checkerbooks Incp, USA'. In the event, though, the New York-based Checkerbooks issued only one Hank Janson novel, a 1949 edition of *Lady, Mind That Corpse* (see facing page), before going out of business. A little later, the Canadian company Weldun Publications brought out, under its Pony Book imprint, an edition of *Honey, Take My Gun*, retitled *Orchids to You* (see above), but this also turned out to be a one-off. By 1951, Frances had assigned the overseas rights in the novels to another New York-based firm, Flamingo Publishing, who that year published an edition of *Smart Girls Don't Talk* as the first issue of an intended ongoing *Hank Janson Detective Magazine* (also above). Once again, though, no further titles were forthcoming.

It was not until 1963 that Hank Janson made a more extended foray into the US market, when Godfrey Gold and David Warburton entered into an agreement with the Derby, Connecticut-based New International Library to publish a series of novels under the Gold Star imprint. Over the next two years, US editions of seventeen of the novels were published – retitled and with extra sex scenes specially written in. All seventeen are pictured over the following pages. Sadly, despite boasting excellent cover art, these Gold Star titles did not sell well enough to merit the range being continued further, and they proved to be the last North American-published Hank Janson books.

Kill Her With Passion (*Crowns Can Kill*) (1963). Art by Harry Barton.

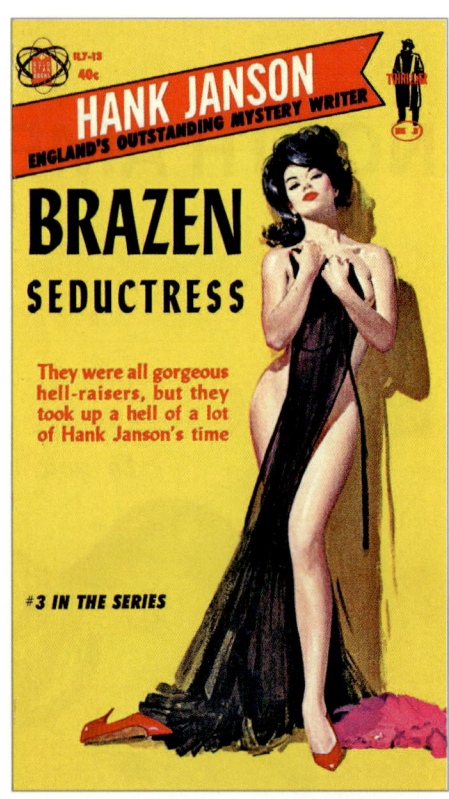
Brazen Seductress (*Ripe for Rapture*) (1963). Art by Robert Maguire.

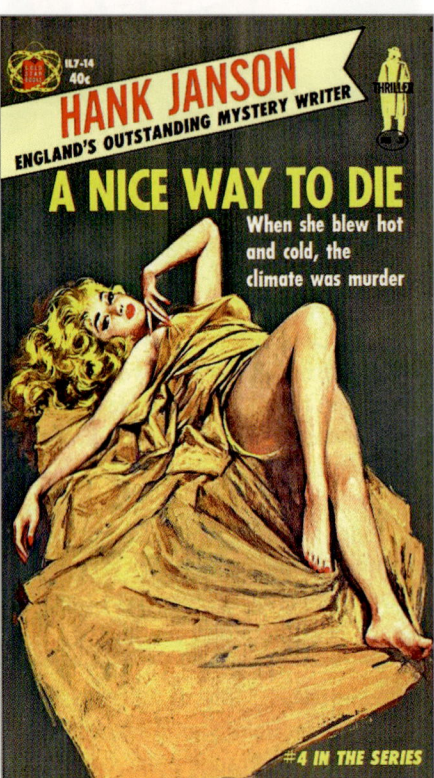
A Nice Way to Die (*Mastermind*) (1963). Art by Paul Rader.

It's Bedtime, Baby! (*Cutie on Call*) (1964). Art by Harry Barton.

Lover (*She Wolf*) (1963). Art by Robert Maguire.

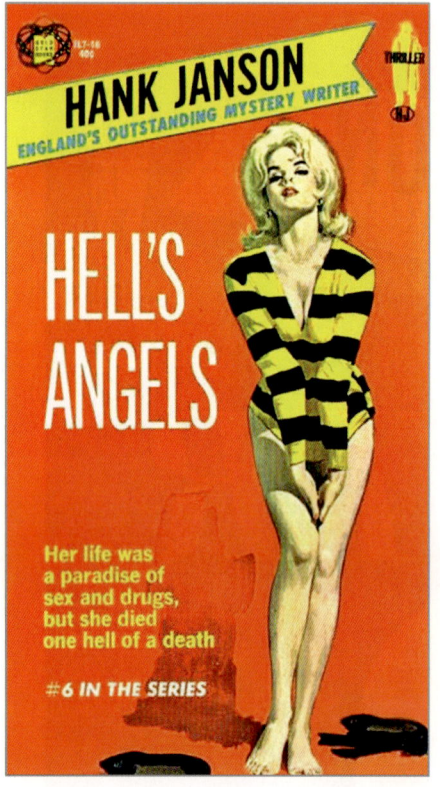

Hell's Angels (*Late Night Revel*) (1964). Art by Robert Maguire.

Hot House (*Venus Makes Three*) (1964). Art by Harry Barton.

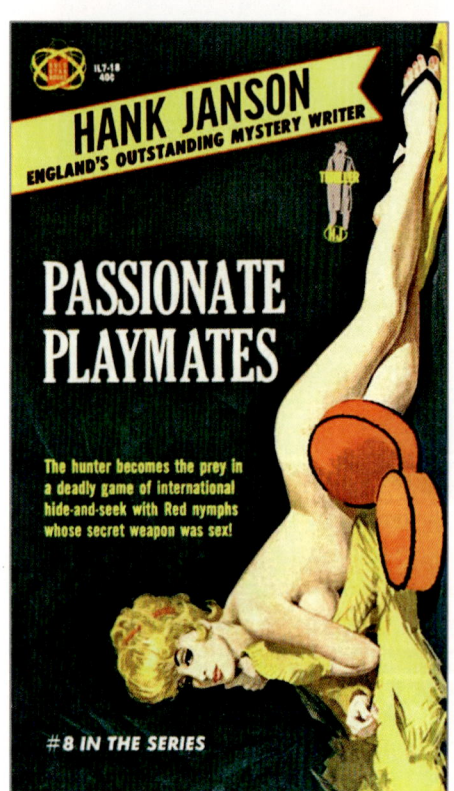

Passionate Playmates (*Go With a Jerk*) (1964). Art by Robert Maguire.

Her Weapon is Passion (*Conflict*) (1964).

NORTH AMERICAN EDITIONS

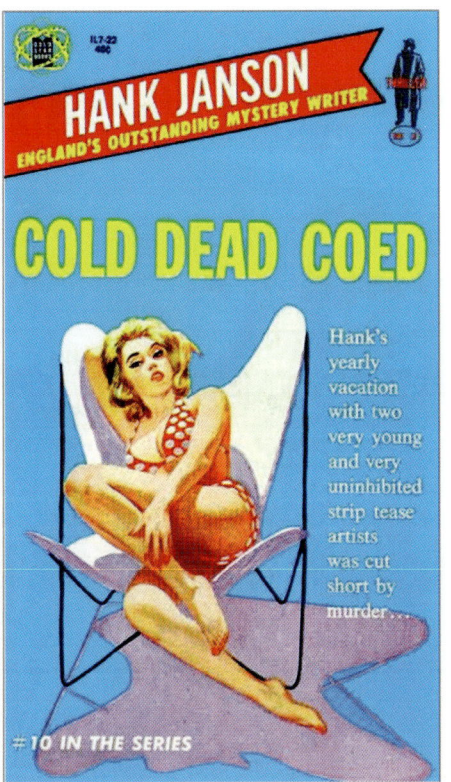

Cold Dead Coed (*No Regrets for Clara*) (1964). Art by Harry Barton.

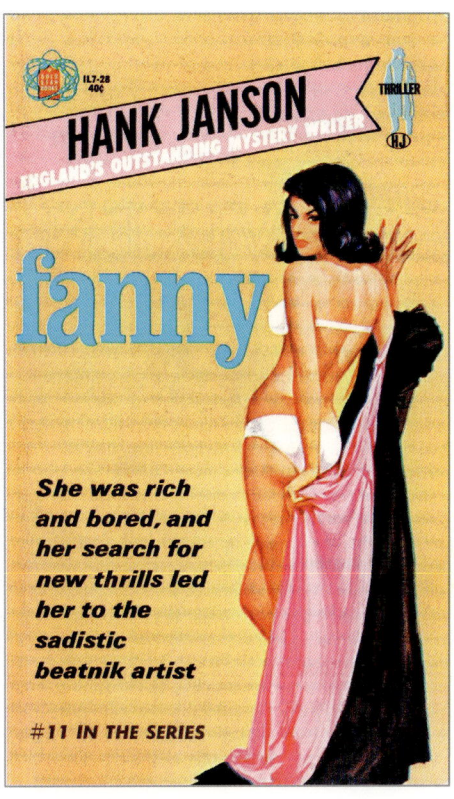

Fanny (*This Dame Dies Soon*) (1964). Art by Harry Barton.

Expectant Nymph (*Murder*) (1964). Art by Robert Maguire.

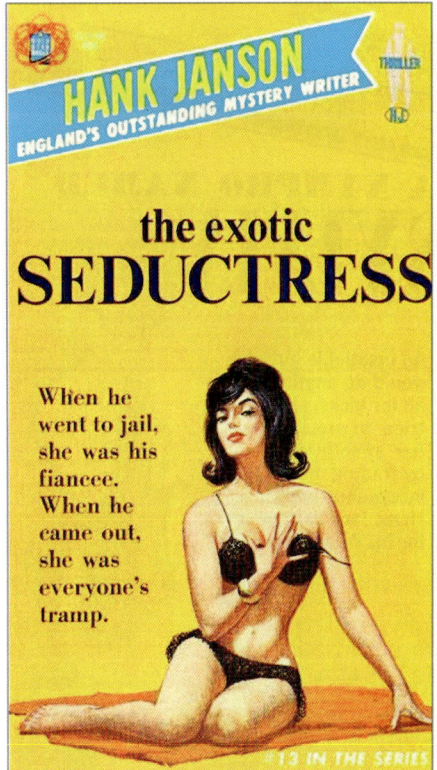

The Exotic Seductress (*They Die Alone*) (1964). Art by Harry Barton.

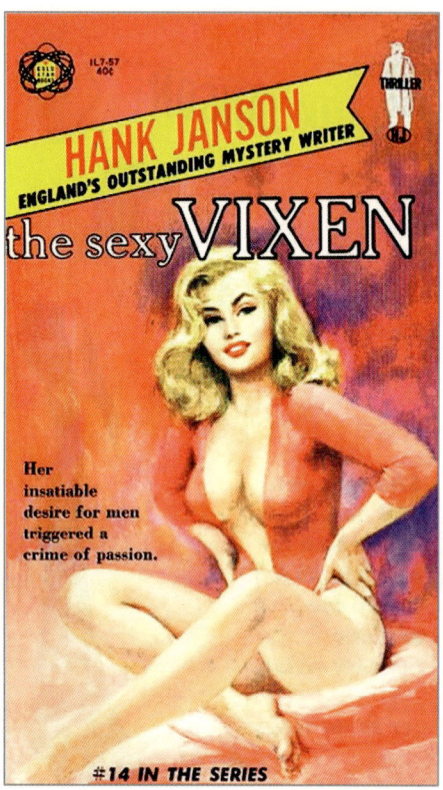
The Sexy Vixen (*Skirts Bring Me Sorrow*) (1964). Art by Harry Barton.

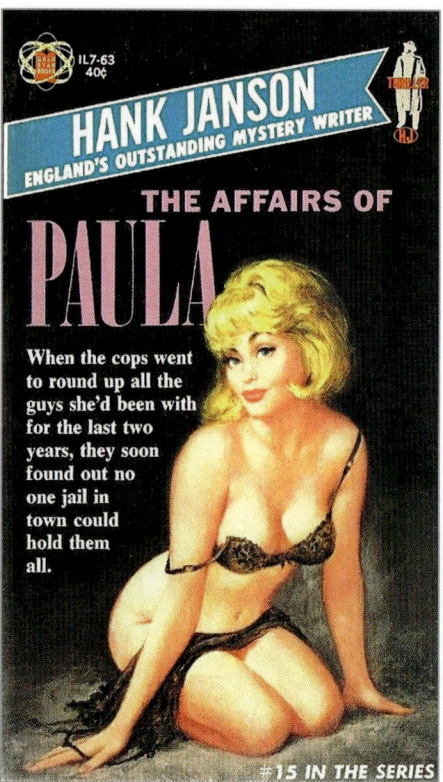
The Affairs of Paula (*Sweet Fury*) (1965). Art by Harry Barton.

A Nympho Named Sylvia (*Enemy of Men*) (1965). Art by Harry Barton.

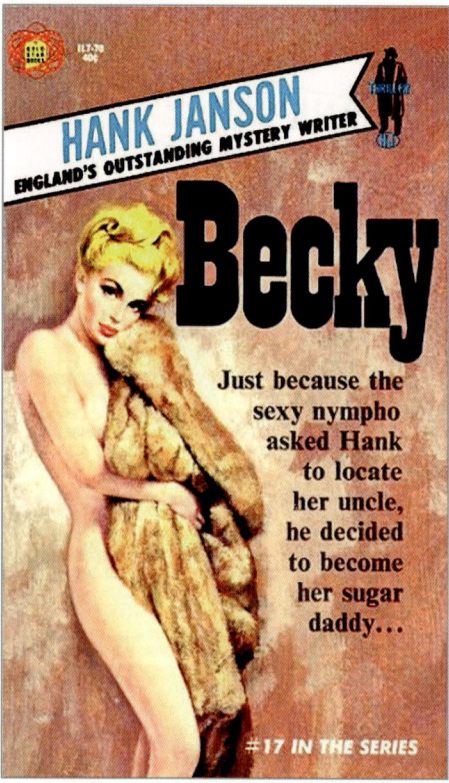
Becky (*Sinister Rapture*) (1965). Art by Robert Maguire.

NORTH AMERICAN EDITIONS

ABOUT HANK JANSON

Hank Janson is about 37. Six feet, three inches tall, weighs about 200 pounds, has close-cropped light brown hair, hard grey-blue eyes with rather heavy brows, a craggy nose, thickish ears, prominent square jaw and fairly full mouth with sound, if rather uneven teeth; face is clean-shaven, scarred in several places. He is very broad and muscular at chest level, still reasonably slim at the waist.

He likes most: beautiful women, Scotch whisky, American cigarettes, good food and wine, and fast driving—in that order; dislikes most: hypocrisy, pimps and other exploiters of women, moral cowardice, racial prejudice, crooked cops—the order depending on the circumstances.

He wears mainly lightweight suits (preferably London tailored), colorful shirts and ties, rubber-soled shoes, and is traditionally pictured as clad in raincoat and fedora with turned-down brim.

He is, of course, single and lived, during the hey-day of his Chicago adventures, in a centrally-placed bachelor apartment. In his most recent stories he has concentrated on his adventures as a free-lancer.

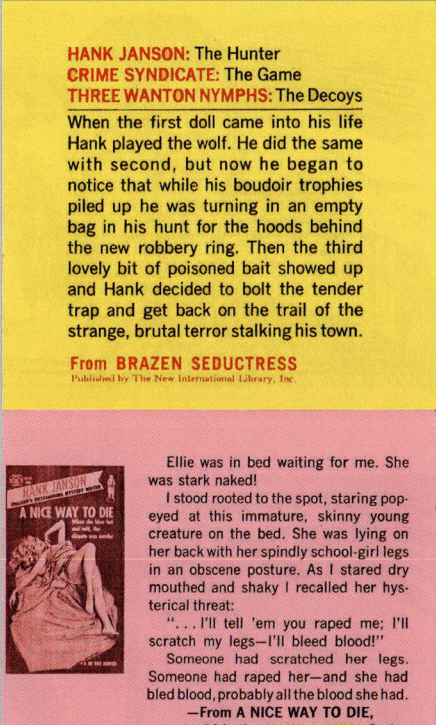

HANK JANSON: The Hunter
CRIME SYNDICATE: The Game
THREE WANTON NYMPHS: The Decoys

When the first doll came into his life Hank played the wolf. He did the same with second, but now he began to notice that while his boudoir trophies piled up he was turning in an empty bag in his hunt for the hoods behind the new robbery ring. Then the third lovely bit of poisoned bait showed up and Hank decided to bolt the tender trap and get back on the trail of the strange, brutal terror stalking his town.

From BRAZEN SEDUCTRESS
Published by The New International Library, Inc.

Ellie was in bed waiting for me. She was stark naked!

I stood rooted to the spot, staring pop-eyed at this immature, skinny young creature on the bed. She was lying on her back with her spindly school-girl legs in an obscene posture. As I stared dry mouthed and shaky I recalled her hysterical threat:

"... I'll tell 'em you raped me; I'll scratch my legs—I'll bleed blood!"

Someone had scratched her legs. Someone had raped her—and she had bled blood, probably all the blood she had.
—From A NICE WAY TO DIE,
Litho. in U.S.A. #4 in the HANK JANSON Series

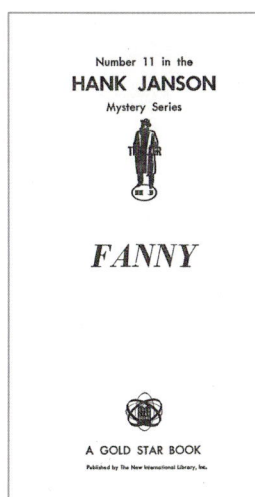

...calls up Hank Janson to make a date, then holds him up and steals his wallet, the hard-boiled newspaperman's curiosity is aroused. When the same girl, after an all-night date, asks Hank to introduce her to an actor, and then murders the actor, Hank is fascinated. When the cops pin the murder on Hank, he is astounded...

Published by The New International Library, Inc.
Litho. in U.S.A.

Top left: the standard biography of Hank Janson that appeared at the front of each of the Gold Star books. Right-hand column: the back covers of *Brazen Seductress* and *The Affairs of Paula*. Bottom left: a typical Gold Star title page. Bottom centre: a back-page advert for Gold Star's other Hank Janson novels, this one taken from *Fanny*.

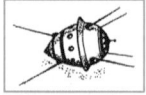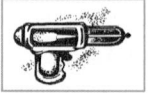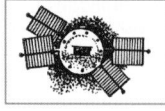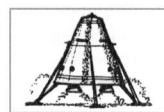

Above: the black-and-white internal illustrations that made for an unusual bonus feature of *Subdolo Attacco*, an Italian translation of the classic-era 'special' *The Unseen Assassin*. (The smaller illustrations were for chapter headings.) This was published in 1961 by the Milan-based Ponzoni Editore under its science-fiction imprint I Romanzi Del Cosmo, or Cosmo for short. The first of these black-and-white pieces bears the signature 'Tor', while the book's colour cover painting – see page 222 – is signed 'Garonzi'. However, as is generally the case with the foreign-language editions, nothing more is currently known about these artists. This edition of *Subdolo Attacco* also included, at the back, an unrelated short story, 'I Docrobots' by Norman Shave, and even a page of cartoons.

FOREIGN-LANGUAGE EDITIONS

Above: Spanish-language translations of the Roberts & Vinter titles *Cool Sugar* and *Delicious Danger* respectively, *Demasiadas Tentaciones* (Colección Apasionada, 17 May 1963) and *Llevame Al Peligro* (Editorial Débora, 1963) are believed to have been the only Argentinian Hank Janson books, the publishers both being based in Buenos Aires.

Between the 1950s and the late 1980s there are believed to have been published somewhere in the region of 800 different foreign-language editions of the Hank Janson novels. Certainly there were too many for all of their covers to be reproduced here. Instead, presented in this section are a selection of examples, arranged on a country-by-country basis.

FRANCE

There were a total of nine French Hank Janson books. The first two (see below) were *Faut Pas Crier, Cherie!*, a December 1952-published translation of *Baby, Don't Dare Squeal*, and *Les 'Jupes' Lui Donnet Du Souci!*, a March 1953-published translation of *Skirts Bring Me Sorrow*. These came from the Paris-based Editions Le Condor, as the first and fourth entries in their Votre Roman Noir, Madame … series. The cover art for both was by Jihel, real name Jacques Leclerc.

Next came *Razzia Sur La Drogue,* apparently an unrelated crime story to which the Janson name was attached (see right), published in 1965 by Editions Bel-Air as part of their Détective Pocket series. The cover artist for this was James Hodges.

The final French titles were six books (see facing page) published between 1966 and 1972 in the L'Aventurier series from Editions 'Fleuve Noir', another Paris-based imprint, with cover art by Michel Gourdon. These were *A La Va-Viet* (*Nerve Centre*), *Fan-Fanfare* (*Fan Fare*), *Yé-Yé Yemen* (*Hot Line*), *Vaudou Veau d'Or* (*Voodoo Violence*), *Ding-Dong Dingues* (*A Girl in Hand*) and, with a cover error in Hank's surname, *Intoxicomani* (*Square 1*).

FOREIGN-LANGUAGE EDITIONS

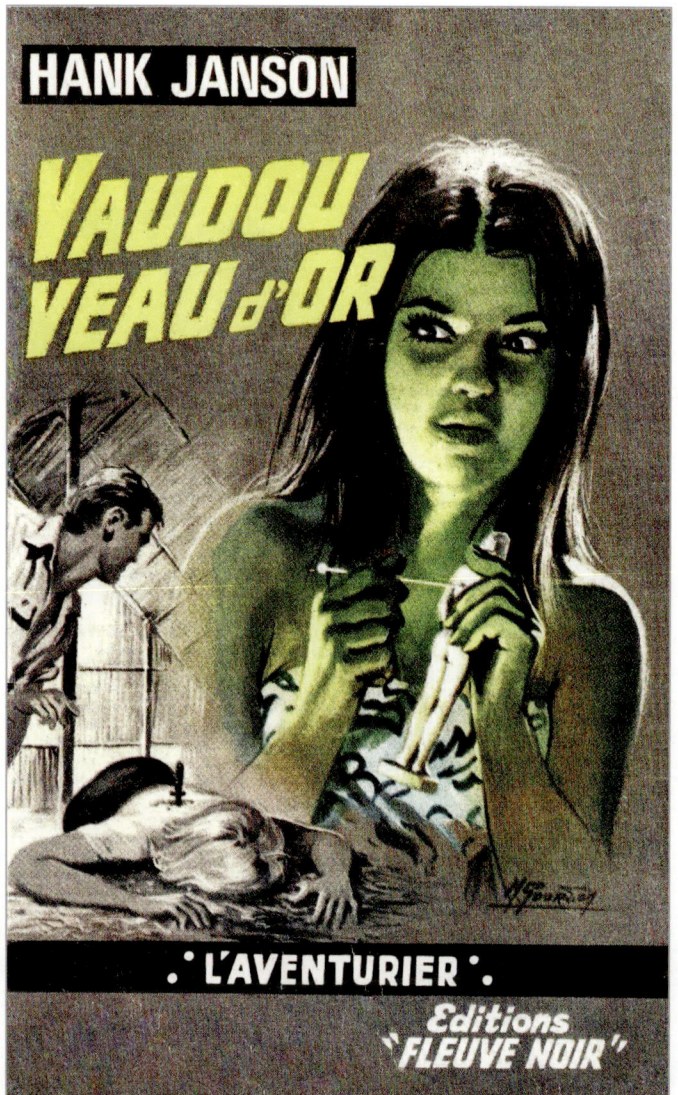

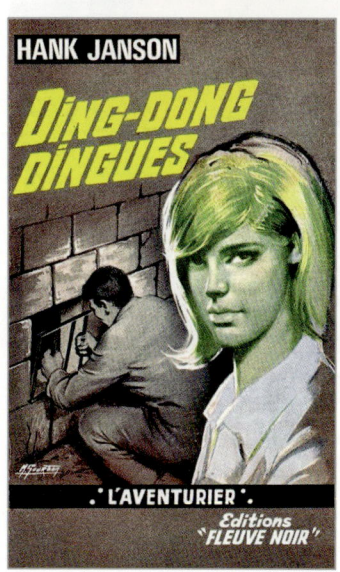
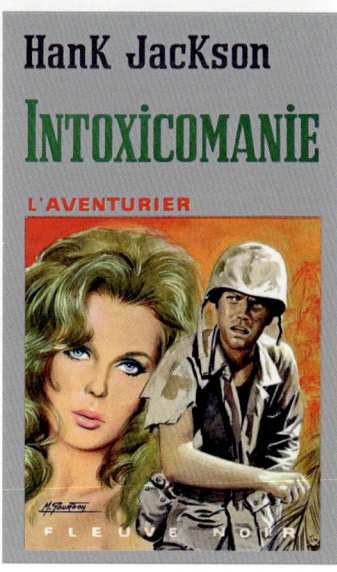

ITALY

Between 1958 and 1961, Hank Janson editions appeared under three different Italian imprints: Cosmo, who had just a translation of *The Unseen Assassin* (see right and page 218); I Gialli Polizieschi Americani (other images on this page); and I Gialli Del Triangolo (facing page). It is unconfirmed exactly how many Janson books there were under each of the latter two imprints, but those shown here would have been most if not all of them.

FOREIGN-LANGUAGE EDITIONS

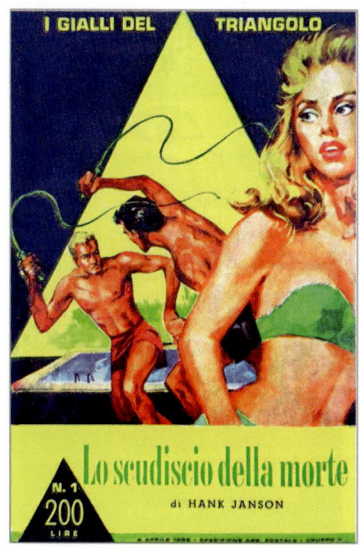
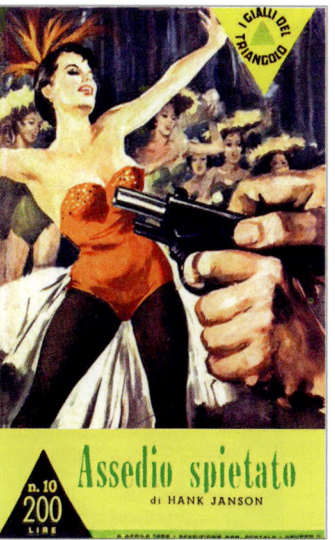

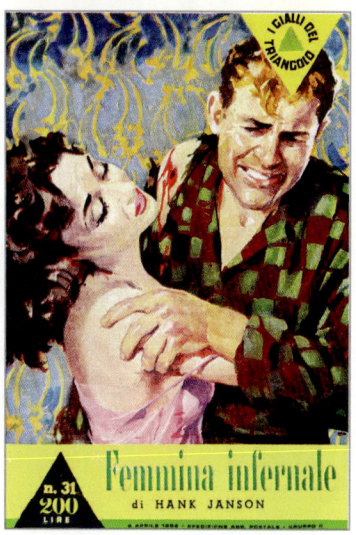

SPAIN

Only a few Hank Janson books were published in Spain. These included, from Edhasa's science fiction imprint Nebulae, 1955 and 1962 editions of *La Violacion Del Tiempo*, a translation of *One Against Time* (see right). From Comercial Atheneum, around 1955, with art by Cerón Núñez, came *Lady, Mind That Corpse*, translated as *¡I Encanto, Ojo Con El Cadáver!* (see front and back covers and title page below). This was presented as part of an ongoing Hank Janson range, but appears to have been the only one.

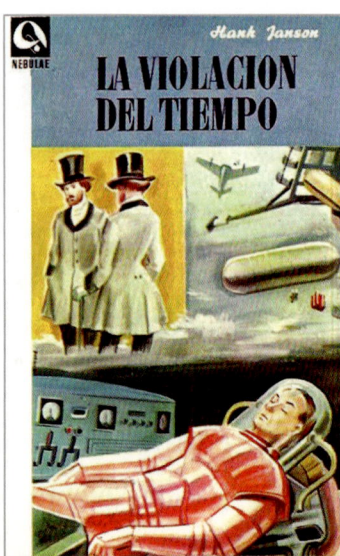

NETHERLANDS

Dutch company UMC published, in addition to their Hilary Brand titles (see page 209), forty-two possibly unlicensed Dutch-language Hank Janson editions, the first of them in 1961 and the last in 1963. These overlapped with the output of another Dutch imprint, Classics Pocket, under which fourteen Hank Janson books saw print between 1959 and 1967. To avoid confusion, or more likely legal action, as some of the novels translated by the two companies were the same ones, UMC gave the author credit on twelve of theirs not to Hank Janson but to Danny Carter, and on a further ten to Frank Stephens (a play on the name of Stephen Frances). Examples of the UMC books are shown from this page to page 227. Their poorly-printed cover artwork was uncredited, and in some cases borrowed compositions or elements from the British range. Examples of the Classics Pocket books, which used a mixture of artwork and photographic covers, can be found on pages 228 and 229.

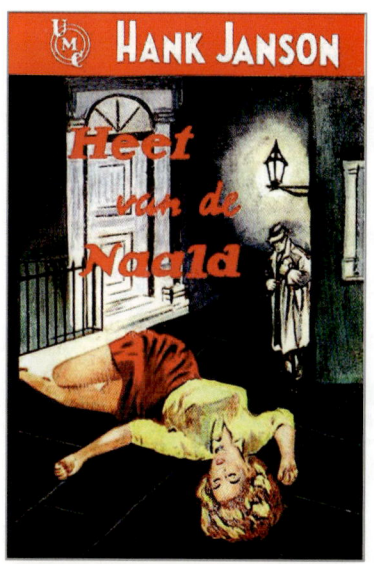

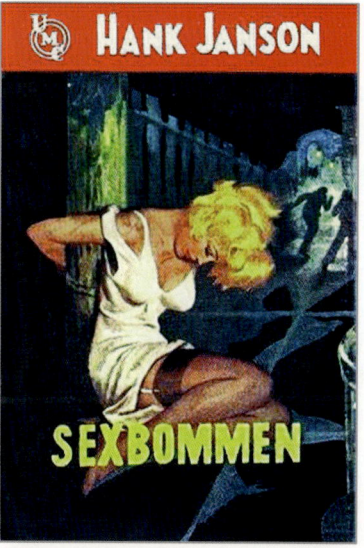

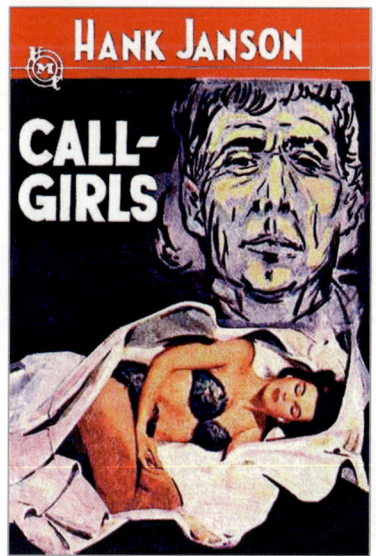

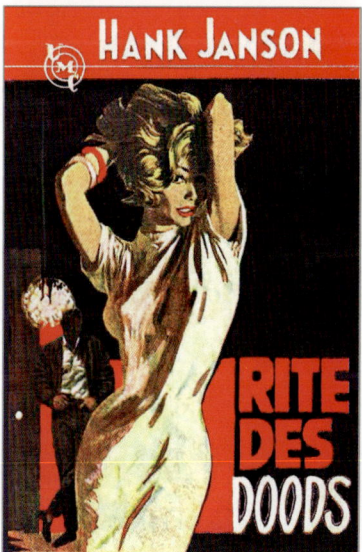

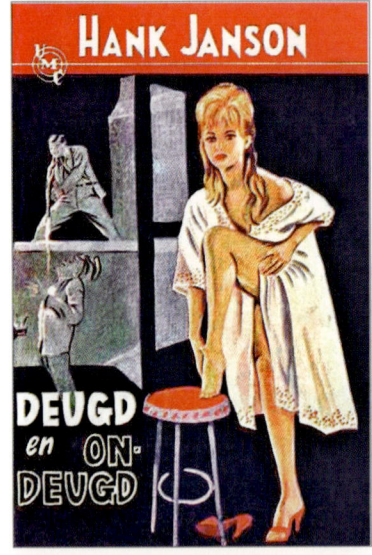

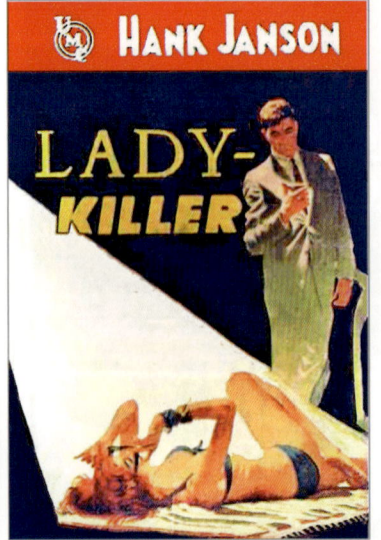

FOREIGN-LANGUAGE EDITIONS

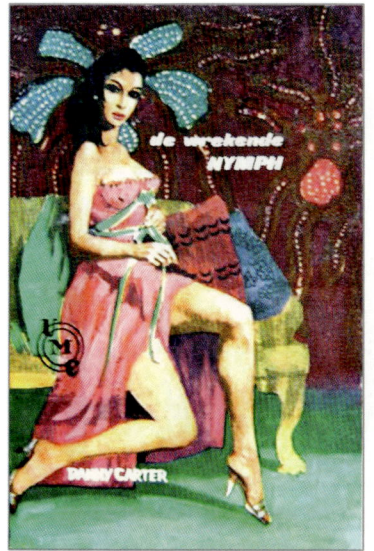

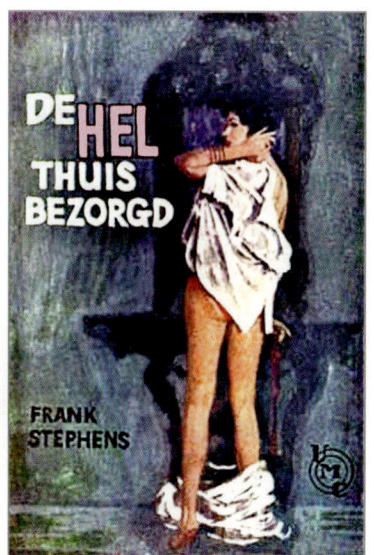

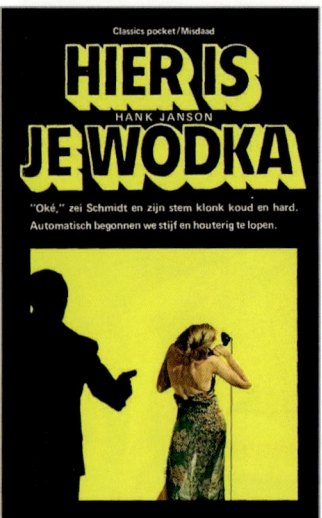
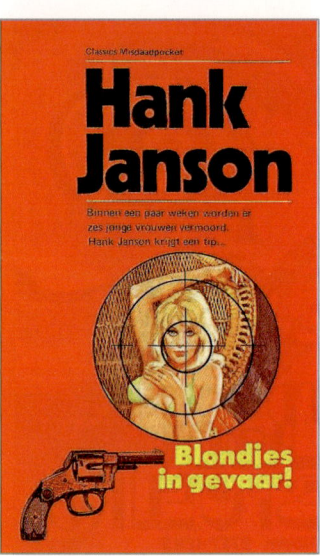
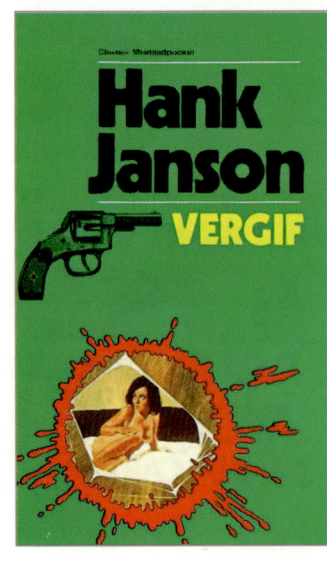

FOREIGN-LANGUAGE EDITIONS

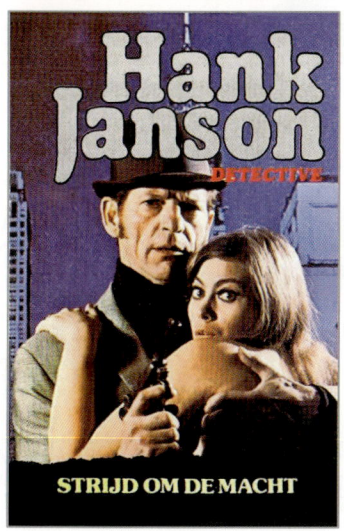
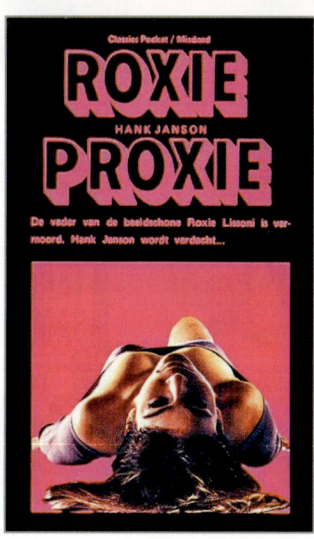

HANK JANSON UNDER COVER

FINLAND

Translation rights in the Roberts & Vinter-era novels were offered widely in Europe. While only a few titles appeared under Dutch imprint Classics Pocket (see previous page), lengthy runs resulted elsewhere. In Finland, the rights were taken up from 1963 by a company called Viihdekirjat, and then from 1980 by Wennerbergs Förlag. Curiously, in these translations, Hank's surname was altered from Janson to Jason. After all of the available titles had been published once, most if not all were issued again with new covers; the series numbered more than 120 by its close in 1982. Both artwork and photographic covers were used; examples are shown from here to page 233. The same images appeared on other Scandinavian and Classics Pocket books too, all being sourced from the same agency. A couple of the pieces were by Robert McGinnis, including one used on the *Deadly Horse-Race* translation pictured below, appropriated from a 1967 US book, *Murder Takes No Holiday* by Brett Halliday.

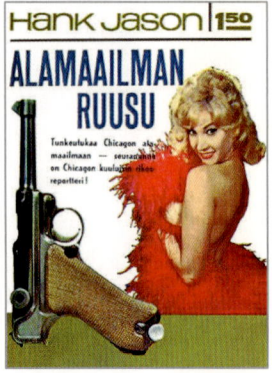

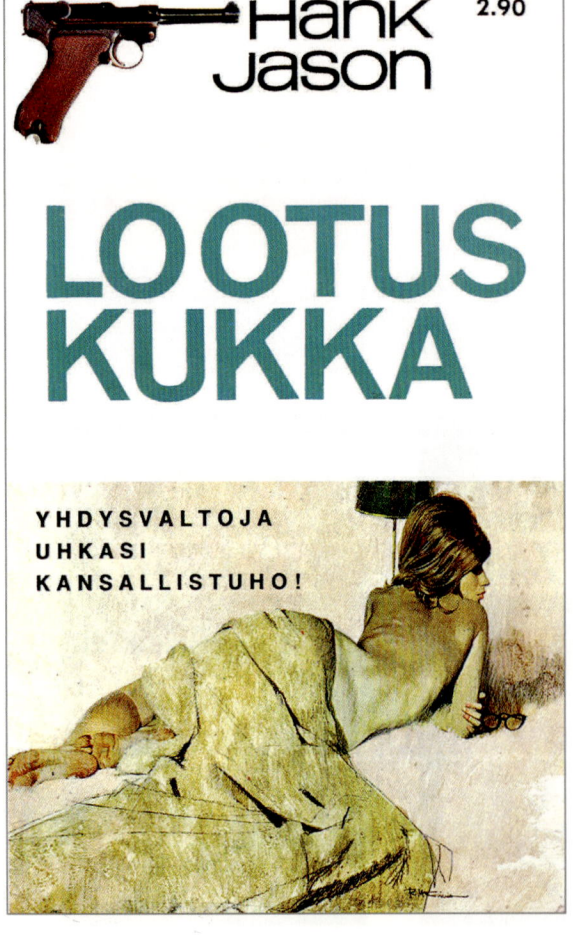

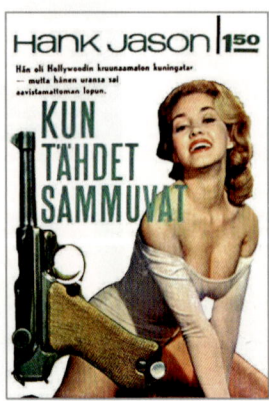
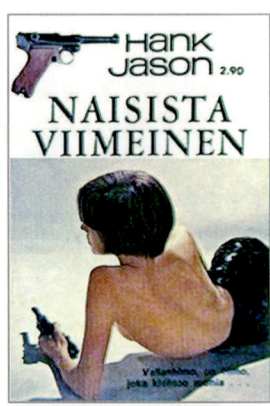

FOREIGN-LANGUAGE EDITIONS

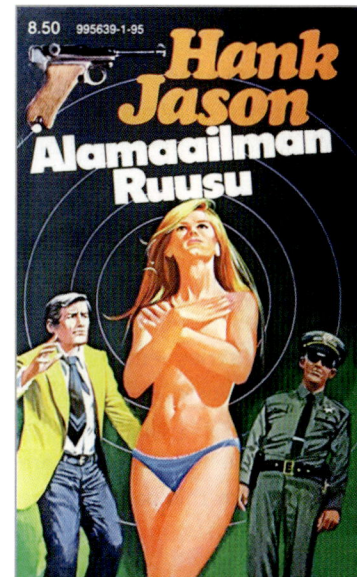
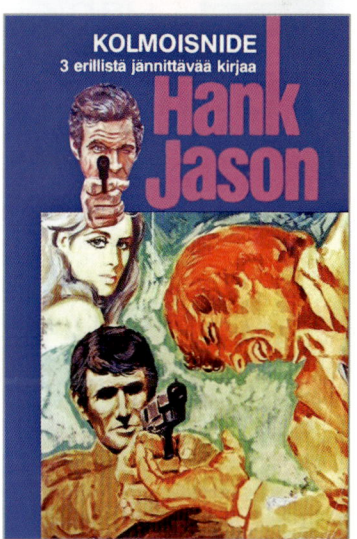

HANK JANSON UNDER COVER

NORWAY

Between 1963 and 1977, over 120 Roberts & Vinter-licensed Hank Janson titles were issued in Norway, initially by the book-publishing arm of long-running magazine *Magasinet for Alle* and then, from 1968, by Forlaget for Alle. As elsewhere in Scandinavia, the latter series entries were simply re-covered reissues, and the cover images all came from the same agency. Examples are pictured from this page to page 237.

  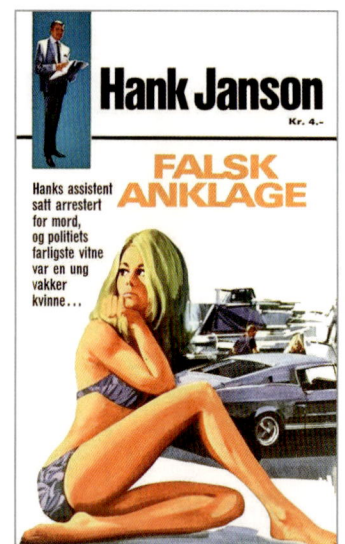

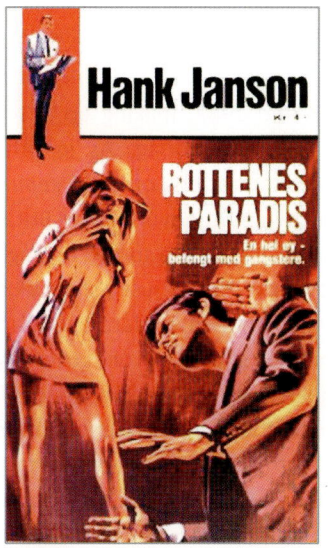

SWEDEN

In Sweden, 74 Roberts & Vinter-licensed titles each saw print twice with different covers between 1963 and 1982, making up a 148-strong series from publishers Wennerbergs Förlag. As in other Scandinavian countries, they included translations of *The Sleeping-Beauty Case* and *Dateline – Death*, the two 1971 novels that in Britain were announced but never published. Examples are shown on pages 239 to 241. While most had a back cover presenting just a short blurb with a detail of the front cover artwork, some in the late 1960s and early 1970s had a larger version of the then standard front cover logo illustration of Hank himself; an example, taken from *Affären Grodnik*, a translation of *Sprung!*, is shown to the right. Some of the 74 Swedish translations even appeared a third time, paired with titles by other authors, in Wennerbergs' extensive Dubbeldeckare (Double Decker) two-novels-in-one-book range – see examples below.

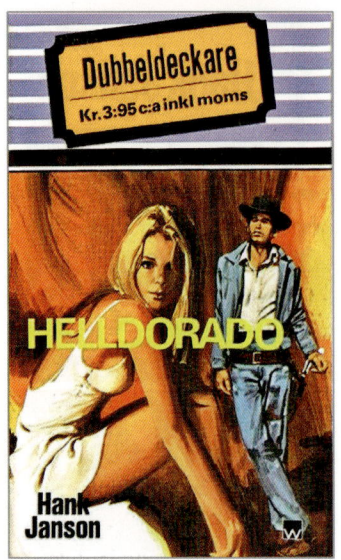

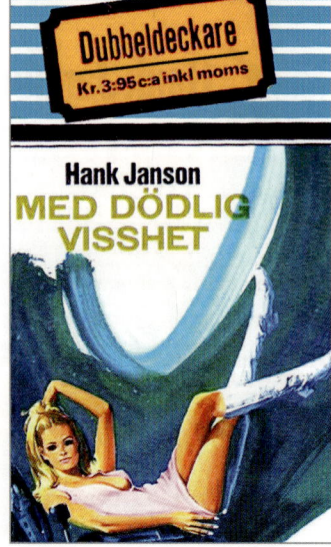

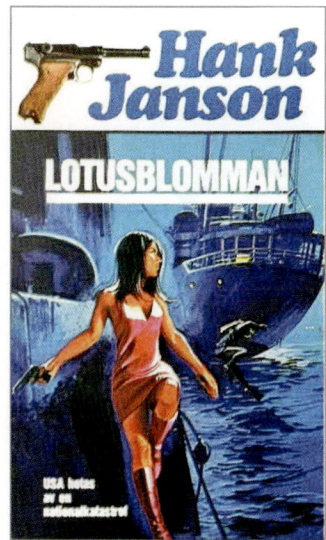

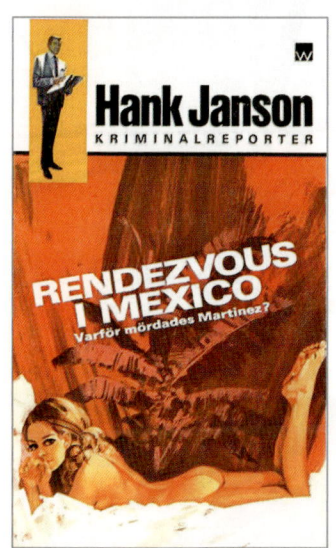
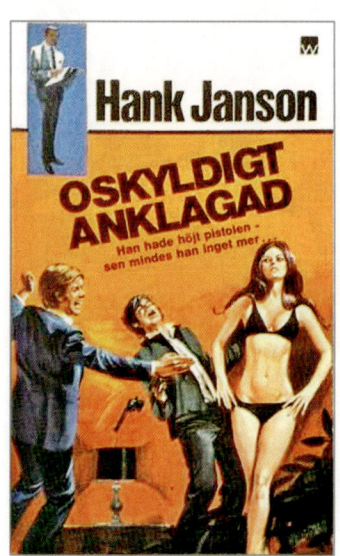

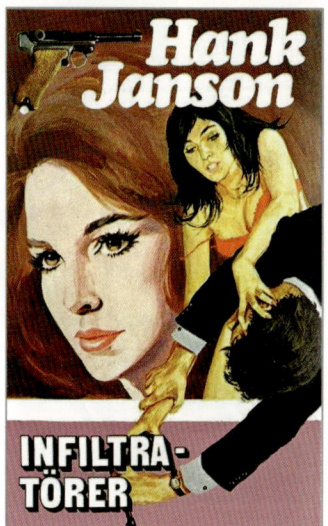

FOREIGN-LANGUAGE EDITIONS

DENMARK

Danish company Winthers Forlag published a numbered series of 227 Roberts & Vinter-licensed Hank Janson titles – although from no. 109 on, all bar one were reissues given new covers, some of them twice. The first came out in 1963, the last as late as in 1988. The covers were again a mix of artwork and photographic, most of them using images also seen on other Scandinavian editions. Examples are pictured below and on pages 243 to 245.

As in Sweden, Winthers Forlag also gave many of these translations an additional reissue, paired with titles by other authors, in their Dobbelt Krimi two-novels-in-one-book range. One example, *Morderisk Jalousi* (*Muderous Jealousy*), the Danish translation of *Mayfair Slayride*, is shown to the right; this was paired with *Det Evige Lig* (*The Eternal Corpse*), a translation of the Carter Brown novel *None But the Lethal Heart*.

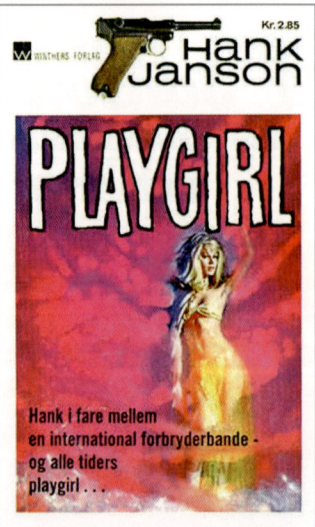

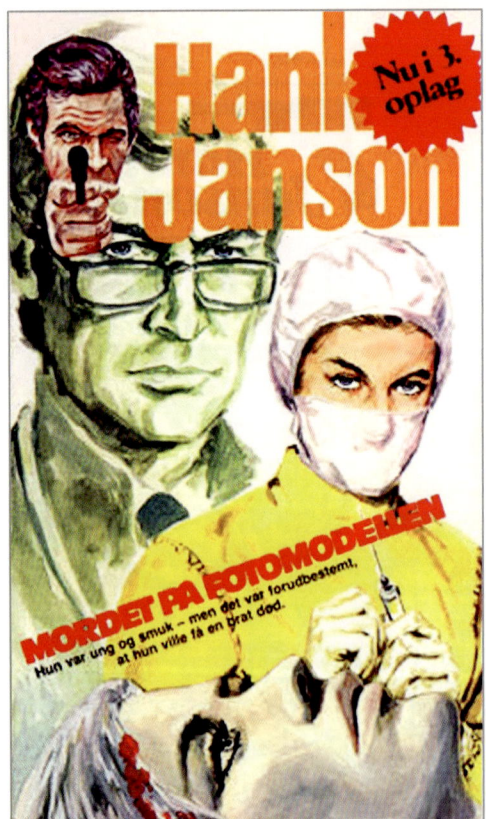

FOREIGN-LANGUAGE EDITIONS

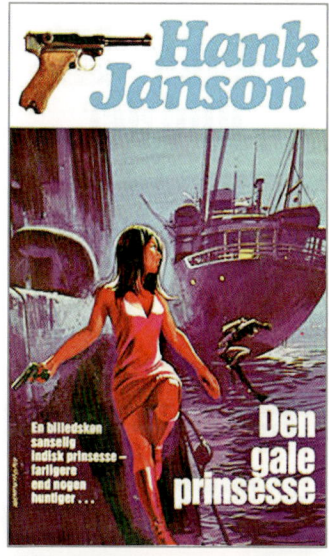
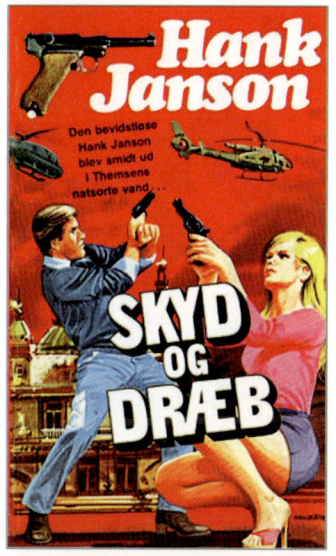

GERMANY

Germany was the last country to see a new range of Hank Janson translations. Between 1968 and 1974, publishers Kurt Desch issued under their Die Mitternachtsbücher (Midnight Books) imprint about a hundred Roberts & Vinter-era titles. The cover images, again a mixture of artwork and photographic, were different from the Dutch and Scandinavian ones; see examples shown over this and the next five pages.

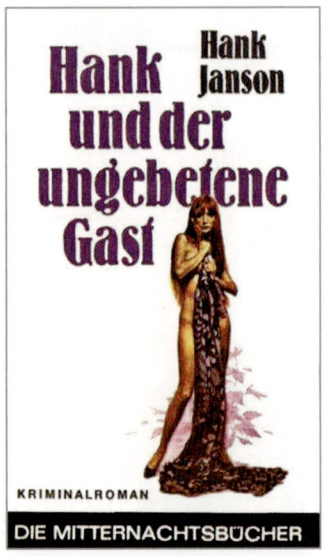
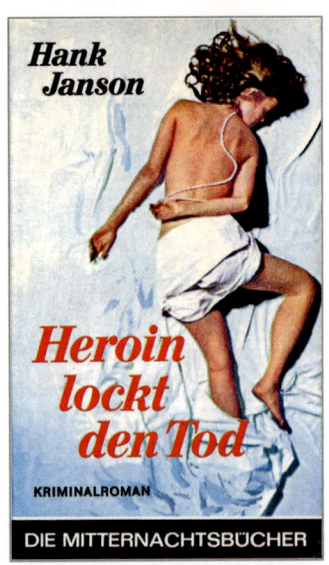

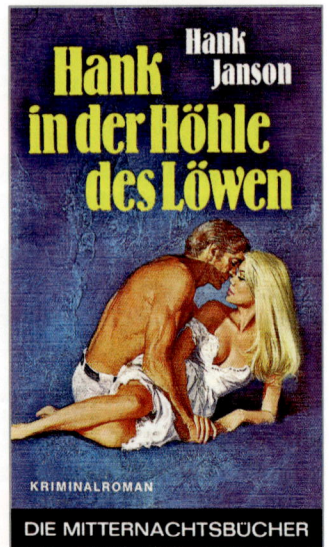

FOREIGN-LANGUAGE EDITIONS

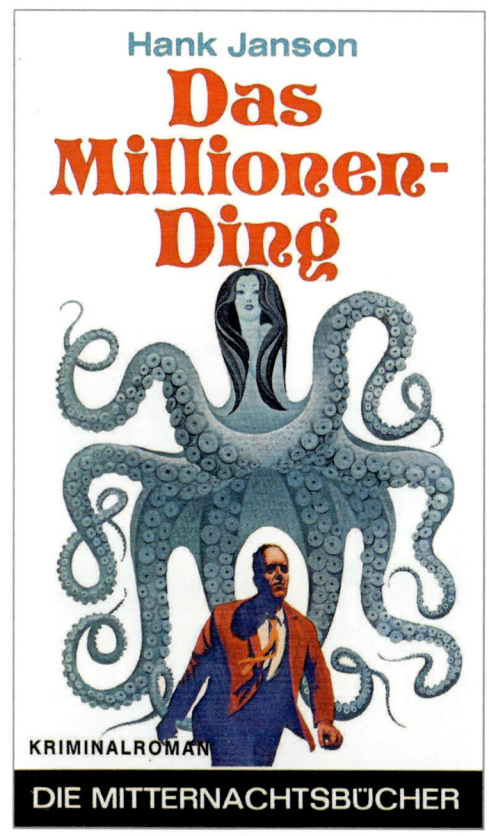

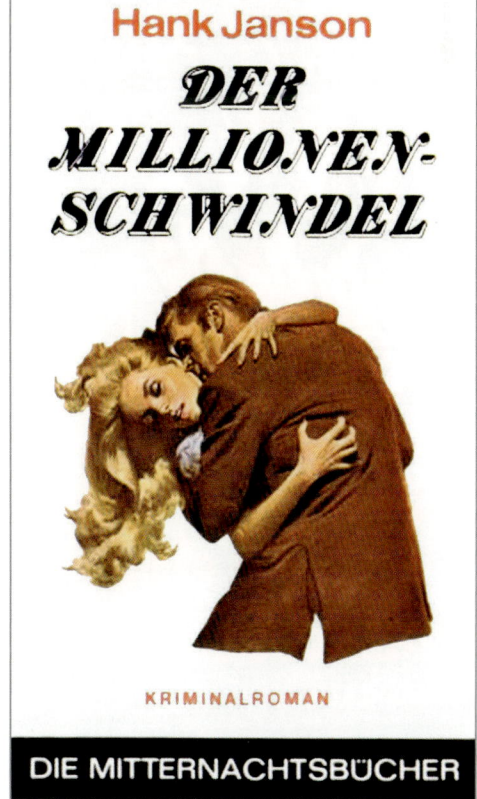

When Dames Get Tough with Scarred Faces & Other Rarities (Telos Publishing, 2004), adapting Reginald Heade's unused cover art from *Slay-Ride for Cutie* (see page 28).

REVIVALS

 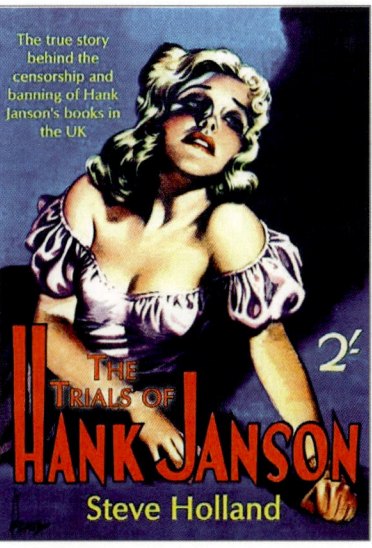 

Left and centre: *The Trials of Hank Janson*, in its original 1991 Books Are Everything edition, with reused art by Fernando Carcupino, taken from the cover of *Quiet Waits the Grave* (see page 127); and in its revised 2005 Telos Publishing edition, with reused art by Reginald Heade, taken from the unpublished cover for *Blonde Dupe* (see page 90). Right: *På Morder Jagt I Hollywood* (*Fan Fare*), a 2021 Danish e-book reissue from Lindhardt Og Ringhof.

The Hank Janson books have always remained popular with lovers of vintage pulp crime fiction, and fondly remembered by those who purchased and enjoyed them back in their heyday. As time has gone by, copies have become increasingly sought-after and treasured by collectors – in large part, of course, due to their sensational cover art. The history of the range, and the life of its creator Stephen Frances, were first detailed by Steve Holland in the original edition of his book *The Trials of Hank Janson*, published in America in 1991 by the Richmond, Kentucky-based Books Are Everything. A revised and significantly expanded edition of that title followed from Telos Publishing in the UK in May 2005, fostering further interest in Hank and his exploits.

Although no new Hank Janson novels have been published since 1971, when Gold & Warburton's Compact imprint came to an end, in July 2003 Telos Publishing launched a range of selected classic-era reissues, complete with suitable Reginald Heade cover art – in some instances pieces that were either censored or left unpublished back in the 1950s. To date, fifteen of these reissues have seen print, but it would be no surprise if more were to follow.

More recently, in 2018, Danish publishers Lindhardt Og Ringhof released, in e-book form only, a large number of reissues of the original Danish-language translations of the 1960s and early 1970s novels; the covers of sixty of these featured adapted versions of Reginald Heade pieces originally painted for the classic-era titles, while those of others used similarly adapted versions of different artists' Alexander Moring-era pastiches of Heade's work. In 2021, this e-book reissue range was relaunched with the release of *På Morder Jagt I Hollywood* (the Danish translation of *Fan Fare*), featuring a new, photo-montage cover (see above).

Over the years, other Hank Janson revivals have been mooted, including even possible television or movie adaptations. So far, nothing has come of these; but who knows what the future may hold? Hank is, after all, a born survivor.

Above left: the 2003 Telos Publishing reissue of *Women Hate Till Death*, adapting Reginald Heade's cover art for the unpublished novel *Woman Trap* (see page 88).

Above right: the Hank Janson range is fondly recalled in a Colin Dunne-written article published in the Saturday 4 January 2014 edition of the *Daily Mail*.

Left: the front and back sides of an advertising card produced by Telos Publishing in 2004 to promote its Hank Janson reissue range. On initial printings, early titles in this range had a coloured border placed around the Reginald Heade front cover artwork, with a caption stating 'A Telos Classic' added at the lower edge. On later printings, this border was dispensed with.

REVIVALS

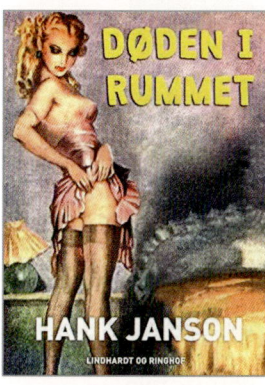  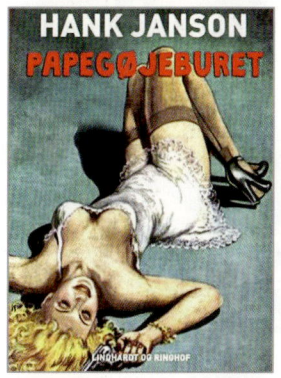 
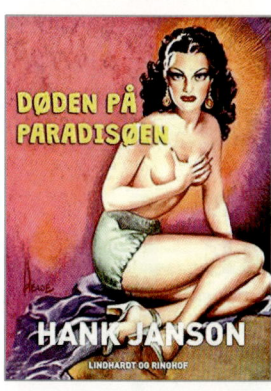 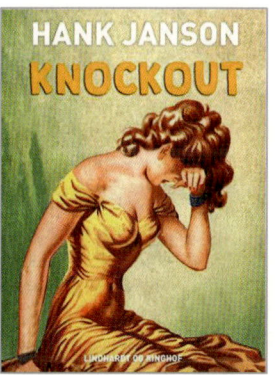  
 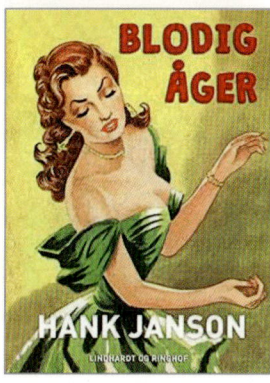 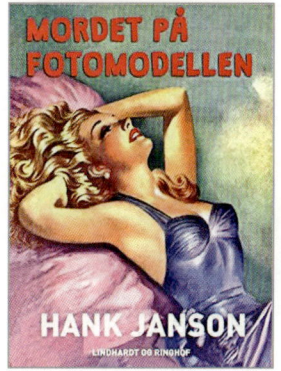 

Above: sixteen examples of the cover images from the Danish-language Hank Janson e-book reissues published by Lindhardt Og Ringhof in 2018. Reused and adapted art by Reginald Heade and others, taken from the classic-era and Alexander Moring-era titles.

ALSO AVAILABLE FROM TELOS PUBLISHING

THE ART OF REGINALD HEADE – SPECIAL EDITION
By Stephen James Walker
320pp. Large format 22cm x 28cm hardback.
Fully illustrated in full colour throughout.
ISBN 978-1-84583-116-5
Published 24 August 2018

THE ART OF REGINALD HEADE – VOLUME TWO
By Stephen James Walker and Steve Chibnall
384pp. Large format 22cm x 28cm hardback.
Fully illustrated in full colour throughout.
ISBN 978-1-84583-155-4
Published 1 November 2020

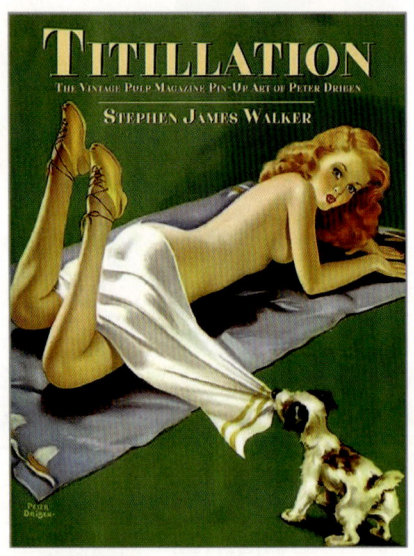

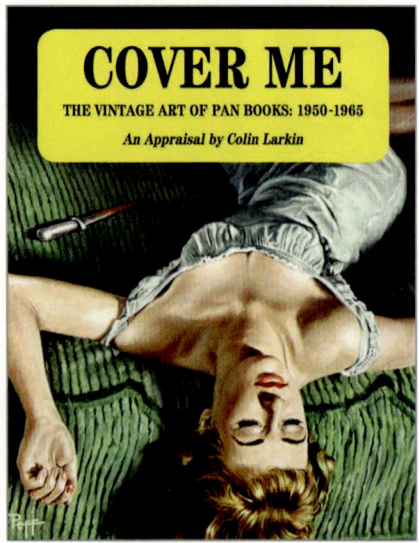

TITILLATION (PETER DRIBEN PULP ART)
By Stephen James Walker
206pp. Large format 22cm x 28cm paperback.
Fully illustrated in full colour throughout.
ISBN 978-1-84583-119-6
Published 19 February 2021

COVER ME (VINTAGE PAN BOOKS COVER ART)
By Colin Larkin
264pp. Large format 22cm x 28cm hardback.
Fully illustrated in full colour throughout.
ISBN 978-1-84583-988-8
Published 1 November 2020